The **Buddhist** Experience

Mel Thompson

seeking religion

Hodder & Stoughton

A MEMBER OF THE HODDER HEADLINE GROUP

Acknowledgements

The publishers would like to thank the following for permission to reproduce copyright photographs in this book:
J Allan Cash: pp17, 25l, 51; Circa Photo Library: pp5tl, 9, 26r, 42, 43, 46t (William Holtby), 36; Corbis: pp5 centre (Mitchell Gerber), 32l (Sakamoto Photo Research Lab); Croydon Buddhist Centre: p5br; Phillip Emmett: pp11, 17 19, 41; The Hutchison Picture Library: pp25r, 44 (Patricio Goycoolea); Christine Osborne/MEP: pp13, 26l, 28, 29l, 46b, 47r (J Worker), 52b (N Dawson); Ann and Bury Peerless: pp6, 37; Popperfoto: p7; The Ronald Grant Archive: p58; David Rose: pp5tr, 22, 23, 27, 39r, 40, 47l, 52t, 54r; Tony Halls/Science Photo Library: p12; Kevin Shaw: 29r; Mel Thompson: pp4, 5bl, 16, 24r, 31, 32r, 38, 39l, 54l, 59, 62.

The publishers would like to thank the following for permission to reproduce copyright material in this book:

Penguin Books Ltd for the extracts from *The Dhammapada*, translated by Juan Mascaro, 1973. Reproduced by permission; Denise Cush for the interview extract on page 54.

> *Note:*
> Dates in this book are given as:
> BCE = Before Common Era
> CE = Common Era

Words in heavy print **like this** are explained in the glossary on page 63.

Every effort has been made to contact the holders of copyright material but if any have been inadvertently overlooked, the publisher will be pleased to make the necessary alterations at the first opportunity.

Orders: please contact Bookpoint Ltd, 130 Milton Park, Abingdon, Oxon OX14 4 SB . Telephone: (44) 01235 827720, Fax: (44) 01235 400454. Lines are open from 9.00–6.00, Monday to Saturday, with a 24 hour message answering service. You can also order through our website www.hodderheadline.co.uk

British Library Cataloguing in Publication Data
A catalogue record for this title is available from The British Library

ISBN 0 340 74771 4

First published 1993
Second edition 2000
Impression number   10   9   8   7   6   5   4
Year   2005   2004   2003   2002

Copyright © 1993, 2000 Mel Thompson

All illustrations supplied by Daedalus, with special thanks to John McIntyre and Steve Parkhouse
Cover photo from CIRCA Photo Library
Typeset by Wearset, Boldon, Tyne and Wear.
Printed in Italy for Hodder & Stoughton Educational, a division of Hodder Headline Plc, 338 Euston Road, London NW1 3BH.

Contents

Buddhism is a way of life based on the teachings of a man who lived in Northern India more than two and a half thousand years ago. His followers called him '**Buddha**', which means 'the enlightened one' or 'the one who is fully awake' because they believed that he had discovered the truth about life.

Buddhism starts with a question:

'Why is there suffering and unhappiness? Can these be overcome?'

Buddhists believe that everyone wants to be happy but that most people don't really know how to achieve true happiness. Some people try to grasp at success, or money, or a career, or someone who will love them. They think that these things will bring them happiness, and sometimes they do. But people can lose their jobs and their money, partners can die or divorce, friendships can end. And all the time, people are getting older. Everyone we know will have to die one day, and so shall we. Life never seems to be quite right, so how can we find happiness?

The teachings of the Buddha aim to help people overcome **suffering** and promote happiness by showing them how to look quietly and carefully at life, to reflect on the way in which things change and to think carefully about what it is that actually makes us happy or unhappy.

Buddhists believe that by doing this they will also become wiser and kinder towards all other living things. They believe that the key to all this lies in thinking and seeing the world in the right way.

● Questions you might want to ask about Buddhism

● WHAT IS ITS PURPOSE?

Buddhist teaching claims to help you become happier. Buddhists say that you can't really understand and love other people until you have started to understand and enjoy being the person you are. Becoming happier yourself is the first step towards making others happy as well.

● IS IT ALL IN THE MIND?

Well, yes. Buddhism is about training the mind to be calm and peaceful, contented and happy. As a result of such inner happiness, it teaches that people will naturally be able to develop heartfelt qualities of kindness and generosity towards others.

● DO YOU HAVE TO BE RELIGIOUS TO BE BUDDHIST?

Buddhism is like other religions because:
- it has temples and shrines where people go to make offerings in front of images
- Buddhists sit quietly in meditation and sometimes chant – often singing the same phrase over and over again
- there are teachings about life and guidelines about how Buddhists should behave
- there are ancient texts that are treated with great respect.

But Buddhism is unlike other religions because:
- Buddhists are not asked to believe anything on trust. They are free to examine all the teachings carefully and come to their own conclusions
- Buddhism does not teach belief in God, nor does it teach that there is no God
- people can practise Buddhism with or without taking part in ceremonies.

So there is no simple answer to this question.

● HOW CAN YOU SPOT THAT SOMEONE IS A BUDDHIST?

Well, take a look at the photos on the next page. What do the people have in common?

▲ Some people are famous for being Buddhist. The Dalai Lama is the leader of the Buddhist people of Tibet, many of whom now live in other countries. He is also seen as a spiritual leader by many other Buddhists worldwide

▲ Other people, like the actor Richard Gere, are famous for some other reason, but also make it clear that they are Buddhist

▲ Other people are seen to be Buddhist by the costume they wear. Here, we can see Buddhist nuns and a monk

◀▶ Most Buddhists, however, are not famous – except among their friends – and they do not wear special clothes. Nor do they come from any particular part of the world. Most Buddhists, in fact, come from the Far East, South East Asia and the Himalayas, but of the two Buddhists shown here, Janet Kovach was born in England and Jacques Seneque in Mauritius, an island in the Indian Ocean

1 Before you start to study Buddhism, write down a list of things you know about it already. Under that, write down any questions that you might want to ask a Buddhist.

2 What things make you really happy? What things make you unhappy? Make two lists. Then:

a) against each of the 'happy' things, put down what that happiness actually depends on. What could prevent you from being happy because of this? (For example: You could be happy when people say you are beautiful or handsome. In that case, your happiness depends on never growing old or losing your good looks.)

b) against each of the 'unhappy' things, write down if there is anything you can do to avoid that unhappiness. (Some things, like a person or animal you love dying, can't be changed. Other things, like being punished for doing something silly, probably can be changed. Think about what you can change and what you can't.)

A Man Called Siddhartha

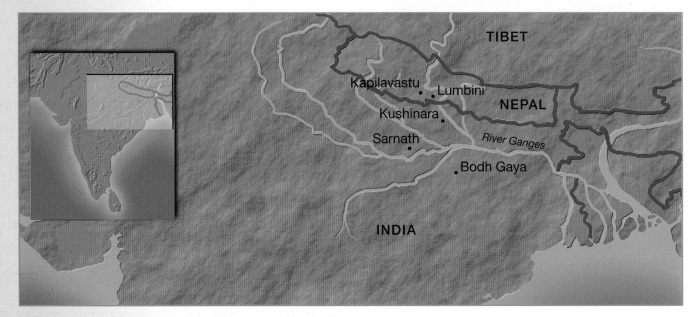

▲ Some places in Northern India associated with the Buddha

The man who was to be called 'The Buddha' was born at Lumbini in the foothills of the Himalayas, in what is now Nepal, about two and a half thousand years ago, and was given the name Siddhartha. His family name was Gautama, so his full name was Siddhartha Gautama (or Siddhatta Gotama, in Pali, a language used for the earliest Buddhist scriptures).

In Northern India at that time there were two kingdoms, but also some areas ruled by local clans. Siddhartha's father, Shuddhodana, was the ruler of one of these clans – the Shakyas. Later, people were to call Siddhartha 'Shakyamuni', which means 'the wise man of the Shakyas'.

So Siddhartha was brought up in luxury, living the life of a local prince, surrounded by everything he could want.

There are many stories about the life of the Buddha. They were passed on by word of mouth for about six hundred years before being written down. They were a reminder of the Buddha's teachings and of his kindness.

According to one story, a wise man called Asita saw Siddhartha when he was a child. He said that Siddhartha would grow up to be a great religious teacher, and that he would give up all his worldly wealth and power.

▲ This stone pillar is at Lumbini. It was put up in about 250BCE by the Buddhist Emperor Ashoka. It says, 'Here was born Buddha Shakyamuni'

Being a prince, Siddhartha was brought up in a palace in his father's capital city, Kapilavastu. He had servants to look after him and give him everything he wanted.

As a young ruler, he was trained in martial arts, such as swordplay, archery and horsemanship. Siddhartha was good at these, but he was also said to be good at sport and the arts. He was even given beautiful young women to take care of him.

At an early age he was married to Yasodhara, a local princess. One tradition says that she saw Siddhartha among other princes at a competition which included sports, martial arts and the singing of love songs! They had a son, Rahula.

Naturally enough, Shuddhodana hoped that his son would want to take over from him as ruler one day, rather than give it all up for religion, as the seer had predicted.

He therefore tried to stop Siddhartha from finding out about suffering and death, in case they led him to think too deeply about life. He also made sure that Siddhartha had every luxury, in the hope that these things would stop him from becoming interested in religion.

But, in spite of all this, Siddhartha was not completely happy. Nor was he content simply to accept what his father had planned for him. He wanted to see what life was like outside the comfortable surroundings of his own little world.

▲ *What is your dream world? Would you like to be like this? Would it make you happy?*

Just enjoy life! Don't think about what might happen as you get older. Troubles always happen to other people.

▲ *Is this good advice? Give your views*

1 Copy out and complete the following paragraph:
The man who became the Buddha was called _____ _____. He was born at _____, which is in _____. He was a prince, who lived in a _____ and had _____ to wait on him. He married _____ and they had a son called _____.

2 Sometimes parents try to stop their children from seeing or hearing about things that might upset them. Do you think this is always a good thing? Write down examples of the sort of things you think should and should not be kept from children. Then compare your lists with others.

3 Parents often have great hopes for their children when they grow up. Do you think this is a good thing? What problems might it create?

4 If you were Siddhartha, would you want to see outside your palace, or would you prefer to stay and enjoy the life of ease? Give your reasons.

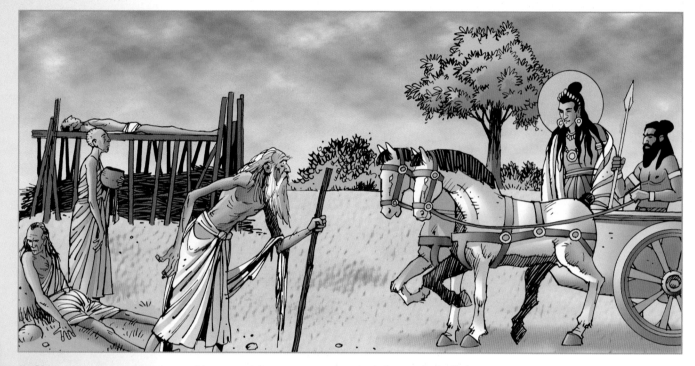

▲ *Siddhartha saw four things: an old man, a sick man, a corpse and a holy man (a Sadhu)*

Whenever Siddhartha went out in his chariot, his father sent servants ahead to try to get all the blind, sick and old people out of sight. But, in spite of this, Siddhartha saw the four things in the picture above. They were to change his life.

After seeing the first three of these – the old person, the sick person and the corpse – Siddhartha realised that he too would one day grow old and die, and there was nothing he could do to stop it. Everything changes and eventually dies; that is a simple fact of life, but thinking about it came as a shock to him.

He was no longer satisfied with his life of luxury, but felt a great love for ordinary people, and wanted to help them overcome their suffering.

The last person he saw was a Sadhu, a holy man who had given up all his possessions to live a spiritual life. Siddhartha felt certain that he should do the same.

He thought about this for a long time. Then, one night, leaving his wife and son in the palace, he asked Channa, his charioteer, to drive him out of the city.

Then Siddhartha got down from the chariot. He cut off his hair, took off his fine clothes and, wearing just a simple robe, he set out on the homeless life. He was twenty-nine years old.

▲ *You are unlikely to see a corpse being carried through the street, but some of the hazards that people face in life are the same now as in Siddhartha's day*

Siddhartha wanted to find meaning and purpose in life and to understand how to overcome suffering. This is how one Buddhist book expresses these feelings:

> ● How can there be laughter, how can there be pleasure, when the whole world is burning? When you are in deep darkness will you not ask for a lamp?
> *The Dhammapada verse146*

For six years Siddhartha lived as an **ascetic**. He accepted the hardships of this way of life and followed the most strict disciplines of the religion of his day (which became what we now call Hinduism). He studied under well-known teachers and then settled to live with five other holy men by the River Nairanjana.

He trained himself to have no food for long periods of time, and then ate only just enough to survive. It is said that he nearly killed himself **fasting** like this. He grew so thin you could see his backbone through his stomach.

Finally, he decided that this discipline was doing him no good. It had not helped him to find the truth about life, so he gave it up. He went down to the river and bathed. Coming back, he met Nandabala, a milkmaid, who offered him some milk rice to eat, which he accepted.

When the other holy men saw him give up his fast, they thought that he would be going back to a life of luxury, and deserted him.

◀ *A Hindu ascetic (a Sadhu) sitting beside the Ganges, in India. Siddhartha tried living this way for six years*

1 Divide a page into four rectangles. Put the title 'The four things that Siddhartha saw from his chariot' and name a different one in each box. Then illustrate each of them, perhaps using newscuttings. Then describe in each box what you think Siddhartha felt when he saw each of these things.

2 Imagine that you are the charioteer Channa. You have left Siddhartha alone to start out on his new life and you are returning to the palace. You will have to explain to the family what has happened and why Siddhartha felt he had to go out into a life of homelessness. Write down how you would explain his decision.

3 Can you think of any examples today of people who have given up money or a regular job, perhaps, in order to go and do something they feel is more important or to live a totally different kind of life? Why do you think someone might do this? Do you think it is a sensible thing to do?

4 'Get real!' Why might you be tempted to say that to a modern-day Siddhartha? What would you mean by it?

▲ *The temptations and Siddhartha's enlightenment. On the right the Buddha is touching the Earth as he is about to become enlightened. He is said to have called on the Earth to witness this event*

In the eyes of everyone else, Siddhartha had failed. He had left his family and the prospect of being an influential ruler in order to follow the spiritual life. Now, after six years, he had realised that the way of discipline was not going to achieve what he wanted. Giving that up, he had been deserted by his five companions.

He had not achieved what he set out to do, but he was still determined to find the truth about life and about how to overcome suffering. He went and sat at the foot of a tree, and vowed that he would not get up until he had found the truth.

Sitting there, many images went through his mind. Some of these were of women, tempting him to be distracted from his **quest** by sexual thoughts. Other images were frightening. But they did not make him change his mind.

He sat under the tree all night struggling with these temptations. As he continued to meditate there, we are told that step by step he started to see everything in a new way. And as dawn approached, he is said to have gained enlightenment, in other words, he is believed to have seen the truth about life.

The word for enlightenment is 'Bodhi', so the tree under which he sat is called the Bodhi-tree (or Bo-tree) – and, of course, someone who has become enlightened is called a 'Buddha'.

From then on, Siddhartha Gautama became known as 'the Buddha'. His followers do not think that he was a god. They describe him as an enlightened human being. In other words, they claim that he was able to see and understand the truth about life.

But what did he see as he sat there all night? What is the vision that makes a person a 'Buddha'?

There is a problem here. In order to know and see exactly what Siddhartha saw, you too would have to be a Buddha! How can you explain something that is totally different from anything you've experienced before? That was Siddhartha's first problem on becoming a Buddha.

For some time he stayed near the Bo-Tree, and considered whether or not it was possible to explain what he had seen. But eventually he came to the conclusion that it was possible, and that there were people ready for his message.

● What did he see?

There are accounts of that night in the Buddhist scriptures, but they are difficult to understand, and the descriptions of what Siddhartha experienced are in terms that would have been more easily understood by people living in India two and a half thousand years ago. But it was something like this:

In his mind's eye he saw everything that had happened in the past, through many, many lifetimes. He also saw millions of creatures being born, living and then dying. He saw life changing and moving on like a great wheel, with individual creatures just a tiny part of that process.

He also saw how all this happens – that everything comes into being because of the conditions that surround it, and when those conditions change, it ceases to be.

He also saw that people suffered because they were always **craving** and grasping at things that were themselves subject to change, hoping that they would provide permanent satisfaction.

The mistake was in seeing people as separate, permanent selves. In reality, he saw everything as constantly changing, part of a pattern of causes and effects that stretched out to the ends of the world.

Siddhartha (or 'Buddha' as he is known from this point on) came to realise that *individual people are not separate from the rest of the world, but are part of it. Everything that arises in their lives comes about because of causes and conditions. The world is always changing, and so are we.*

Buddhists believe that everyone can eventually achieve enlightenment. Some say that everyone has a 'Buddha nature' within himself or herself. Siddhartha is usually described as *the* Buddha, because Buddhists see him as the first to have become enlightened in this way. They also respect him as a great teacher, helping others to understand life, and to make progress towards their own enlightenment.

1 Illustrate the main events in the Buddha's life – from birth to enlightenment. Against each of your drawings, say why it is important for an understanding of the Buddha and what he taught.
2 Many doubts and temptations arose in Siddhartha's mind as he sat beneath the Bo-tree. What doubts do you think he would have had? (Think about his life.)
3 Have you ever felt determined to do something even if everyone else thinks you are wrong? If so, describe how you felt. If not, describe how you think you might have felt. Do you think it takes courage to go on?
4 Although you can't understand it fully without being enlightened, try to put in your own words something of what the Buddha is said to have 'seen' as he became enlightened. Do you think it makes sense?

◀ *This is the oldest authenticated living tree, and is said to have been grown from a cutting taken from the original Bo-tree*

The Buddha now started on a life of teaching. He wanted to help others to achieve enlightenment, and to be freed from suffering.

Buddhist teaching is usually called 'Dharma', which is the **Sanskrit** word for teaching.

Here are some of his most important teachings:

● The Three Universal Truths

1 ANICCA (EVERYTHING CHANGES)

▲ *At one time you were a baby, unable to speak. You may live to be old. Your life will change, and there is nothing you can do to stop it – that is part of what Buddhists mean by 'Anatta'*

Everything in the universe depends on other things for its existence. From the smallest atom to the largest galaxy, things are always changing. If conditions are right, they come into existence; if conditions change, they cease to exist. Life on Earth depends on air, water and the heat of the sun. If any of those things changed, human life would stop. Each thing depends on everything else.

2 ANATTA (NO PERMANENT SELF)

Nobody stays the same from birth to death. Your body grows older, your mind develops. Even your personality changes. Some things happen by chance, but others depend on your own choice. If you try to cling to a fixed idea of yourself, it will lead to conflict and suffering in this ever-changing world.

3 DUKKHA (SUFFERING)

Because everything changes and dies, the Buddha taught that life can never completely satisfy us, and that makes us suffer. Even if we had everything we wanted, there would still be part of us that wasn't really happy. This is what leads people to look for something more in life. If we feel bored or unhappy, it could be that this part of ourselves is trying to tell us something.

▲ *If you've ever felt like this, you know what dukkha means*

Buddhists do not see these 'Three Universal Truths' as in any way sad or depressing. By understanding them, they believe that they can achieve a new way of life that offers real happiness.

● The Four Noble Truths

If you are sick and go a doctor, you want to know:
1 what is wrong
2 what has caused your illness
3 what will cure it
4 how to get treatment.
The Buddha's teaching can be set out in the same way, as a cure for the world's illness:

1 ALL LIFE INVOLVES SUFFERING

The illness is Dukkha. Buddhist teaching aims to help people understand and overcome it.

2 THE ORIGIN OF SUFFERING IS CRAVING

The cause of the illness is an unhealthy craving for life, for pleasure, and for money. The Buddha taught that this craving makes people frustrated and unhappy.

3 IF CRAVING CEASES, SUFFERING WILL ALSO CEASE

If a person can enjoy life without craving or grasping for things, he or she can avoid suffering and live happily. The cure for life's illness is to get rid of craving.

4 THE MIDDLE WAY

The Buddha had lived a life of luxury, and had also tried hardship and poverty. Neither had brought him happiness or overcome suffering. He therefore taught a 'middle way' between these extremes. Buddhists believe that, by following his teachings, they can be cured of their craving and find happiness.

> Buddhism aims to increase happiness, and that means enjoying life. The secret is to enjoy things without craving them or trying to hold on to them.

▲ The Buddha spent many years travelling around Northern India teaching all who came to him. This photo is of Sarnath, where he is said to have started his teaching

In many of the stories about his teaching, someone comes to the Buddha with a problem, he listens to what they have to say, asks questions and then gives advice that will help them to see life differently. In other words, he acts like a doctor dealing with people's religious and personal illnesses.

Some who come to him are wealthy rulers (he knew most of the ruling families in the area), others are poor. Some are ascetics, living under strict religious discipline, others are simple householders.

His teaching is full of surprises. Sometimes those who are Brahmins (the most important of the castes) are criticised, and those who are humbler, but caring for others, are praised.

---

1 a) Write down what each of these means: Anicca, Anatta, Dukkha.

b) Write about something in your own life – a feeling, perhaps, or an event – to illustrate each of these three things.

2 Use the Buddha's Four Noble Truths as a pattern to explain:

a) to a young child why he or she might feel sick after too much food at a party

b) to a middle-aged person who, desperate to make a fortune, has risked all his or her capital on the stock exchange and is now bankrupt, why he or she is suffering.

c) Then think up another situation of suffering and explain it in the same way.

3 'Don't expect anything, and you won't be disappointed!'. That is NOT what the Buddha meant by saying that suffering is caused by craving. Explain in what way his teaching is different, and why it may be quite natural and healthy to enjoy things.

The Noble Eightfold Path

8 By training your mind, you will gradually get rid of hatred, greed and ignorance, so that you can experience joy and peace.

1 Before starting on the path, you know that life involves suffering and change. You also understand that the Dharma offers you a way to overcome suffering and live happily.

7 Become more aware of those around you, and of your own feelings – don't live in a dream world, but see things as they really are.

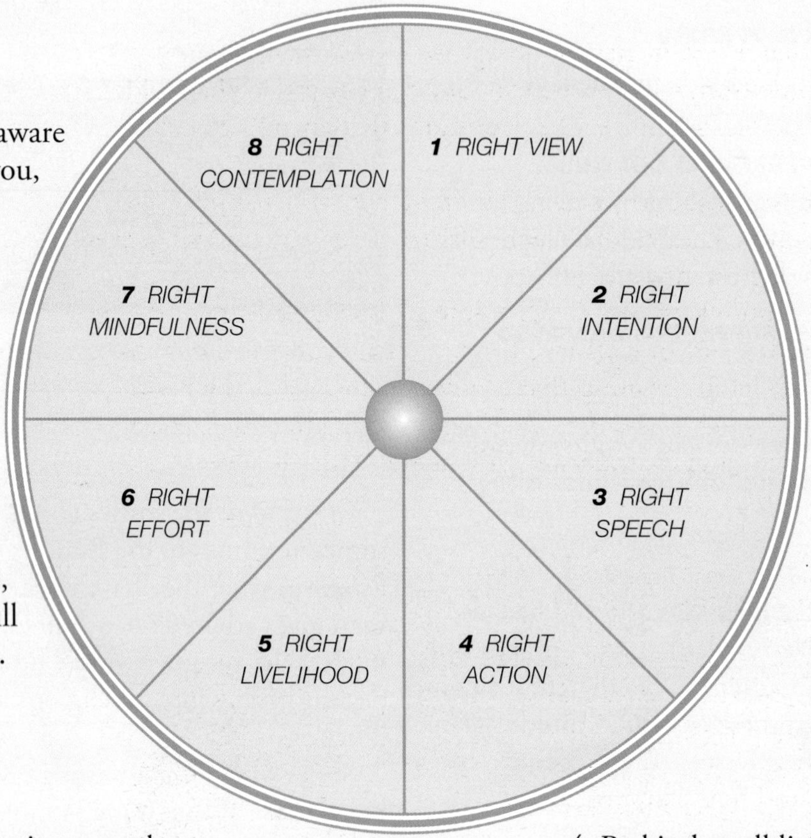

2 You need to commit yourself – just thinking about it is not enough!

6 Don't think harmful thoughts, try to feel goodwill towards everyone.

3 Speak the truth, and speak in a positive and helpful way.

Diagram: wheel divided into eight segments

- 8 RIGHT CONTEMPLATION
- 1 RIGHT VIEW
- 7 RIGHT MINDFULNESS
- 2 RIGHT INTENTION
- 6 RIGHT EFFORT
- 3 RIGHT SPEECH
- 5 RIGHT LIVELIHOOD
- 4 RIGHT ACTION

5 Earn your living in a way that reflects Buddhist values – for example, don't cheat or hurt others by what you do.

4 Be kind to all living beings; be generous; be content; be truthful; keep your mind clear.

Buddhists often refer to their religion simply as 'practising the Dharma'. Buddhist teaching is like a path to be followed, leading a person towards greater contentment and happiness. It takes the 'middle way' between luxury and hardship.

The path can be set out as shown in the diagram above. Although it has eight separate 'steps', they are not taken one after the other. The Buddhist way of life involves all of them.

The first two steps are necessary for people to take the teaching seriously. They must be aware of what the Buddhist path offers, and feel that they really want to follow it.

The next three steps give practical advice for how to speak, act and earn a living. For many people, this is the most straightforward way to start living as a Buddhist.

The last three train the mind to think and feel in a positive way. They help people to take notice of everything that happens around them, and to develop happiness and goodwill towards all creatures.

● Conditions

How does the Noble Eightfold Path work? Buddhists do not believe in a god who will reward them for following the path, so how do they know it will lead to happiness?

The Buddha taught that everything happens as a result of conditions. If you give a plant water and sunshine it will grow. Without them, it will die. So Buddhist teaching is not something that you have to believe or learn in order for it to work, it is simply advice about the sort of conditions that may benefit your life.

Buddhists believe that everyone has the ability to develop wisdom and friendliness. These come from within a person, not from outside. The Noble Eightfold Path simply offers a guide to the conditions that encourage them to grow.

People can be so different. Some people seem to be naturally happy, even when they are having difficulties in their lives. Others are always moaning, even if life seems to be treating them well.

Buddhist Dharma cannot stop people becoming ill, breaking a leg, or dying; these are all features of the sort of world we live in. What it does claim to do is to help them to develop habits of mind that enable them to enjoy the positive things that life brings without grasping or holding on to them, and to cope with life's difficulties by trying to understand them and without adding to them by becoming bitter or hateful.

● A threefold plan of action

Sometimes the Buddhist path is described as the 'Triple Way' of Morality, Meditation and Wisdom.

Morality – how you treat others, following the Buddhist guidelines for life.

Meditation – how you calm your mind, so that you can think clearly, notice what is happening around you, and be aware of your feelings.

Wisdom – how you reflect on the nature of life, how everything changes, and how everything is inter-connected in a huge pattern of conditions.

Each of these is linked to the other two. For example:

- If you do something wrong, your mind might well become troubled as a result, perhaps by feeling guilty or worried about being caught. But if you have treated someone else badly, it means that you do not really understand what life is about, and what will bring happiness.
- If your mind is racing or muddled, you are unlikely to know the right thing to do.
- If you are confused about what life is about, you are unlikely to behave well towards others, or be calm and contented.

▲ *People in similar circumstances can be so different. What's the secret?*

1 Design a poster setting out the Noble Eightfold Path. You could do it as a wheel, or as a path of steps. Do a drawing for each of the steps.

2 **a)** Write down your ambitions, and against each one say what training you would need in order to achieve it.

b) Explain in your own words the Buddhist idea that in order to grow as a person you have to create the right conditions.

Karma

Buddhists believe that everything we do has an effect on us. Each action helps to decide whether we're happy or unhappy in the future. These actions are called **karma**. If you do a helpful or kind action, you will benefit. If you hurt others, then you have to live with the consequences.

Karma is not a system of rewards or punishments imposed on us. It's a simple fact of life. This is how one Buddhist describes it:

> ● I think of the Law of Karma as simply 'Actions have consequences'. If you say a friendly word to someone, or point out their good qualities, that strengthens your friendship. Later they may say something positive back to you. Although you don't do it in the hope of that, it's the natural result of your good karma.

▲ *It's not quite that simple! We don't always see the long-term effects of what we say or do*

Look at the verses from the Dhammapada, an early Buddhist book, in the box. They suggest that whatever you think or do today will make you what you will be tomorrow. Therefore, if you hate someone and go out and injure or kill them, that other person is not the only victim of what you have done. You too will have to live with the consequences. Perhaps you will be caught and punished. But even if you escape external punishment, Buddhist teaching says that you carry around in your mind the results of what you have done. That action has made you a bit different. It is bad karma.

Of course, you always have opportunities to change, and to practise those things that are good karma, and you will then benefit as a result.

> ● Remember, karma is NOT a law imposed on you from outside, it is simply a matter of cause and effect.

● What we are today comes from our thoughts of yesterday, and our present thoughts build our life of tomorrow: our life is the creation of our mind.

... If a man speaks or acts with an impure mind, suffering follows him as the wheel of the cart follows the beast that draws the cart.

... If a man speaks and acts with a pure mind, joy follows him as his own shadow.

The Dhammapada verses 1, 2

But what happens to all your good and bad karma when you get to the end of your life?

In India, most people believe in reincarnation; that after death a person is re-born into another life. It was the same in the Buddha's day, although the Buddha himself did not encourage people to think about such things, about which people could not know anything for certain.

Most Buddhists therefore believe that the karma which has not already had its results in this life, may have results in future lives after their present life has ended. Exactly how this might happen, of course, is something we cannot know.

Beliefs and ceremonies

But do you have to take part in religious ceremonies in order to follow this 'middle way'?

The Buddha argued that, if someone had been shot, it was more important to pull out the arrow than argue about what kind of arrow it was, or from what kind of bow it had been shot.

Just pull it out.

In the same way, it was more important to help people to overcome suffering than to argue about religious ideas, like whether or not God exists. Therefore Buddhist teaching does not include belief in God.

The Buddha warned his followers not to rely on religious beliefs and ceremonies. They do not work automatically, as if by magic. What matters isn't the ceremony itself – it's the attitude of the people taking part.

He also taught that it was more important to follow his teachings than merely to be able to discuss religious ideas. Buddhist Dharma is something to put into practice, not just to talk about.

This is how the Dhammapada puts it:

> ● If a man speaks many holy words but he speaks and does not, this thoughtless man cannot enjoy the life of holiness: he is like a cowherd who counts the cows of his master.
>
> Whereas if a man speaks but a few holy words and yet he lives the life of those words, free from passion and hate and illusion – with right vision and a mind free, craving for nothing both here and hereafter – the life of this man is a life of holiness.
>
> *The Dhammapada verses 19, 20*

▲ *This photograph shows Buddhists taking part in worship by making offerings at a shrine. A Buddhist thinks that any benefit gained from this is in the mind of the person who does it*

1 Write down two actions and their likely consequences. One should show karma producing good results, the other should lead to bad ones.
2 Look at the illustration of the man shot by an arrow. Can you think of any other situation where doing something to help is more important than discussing what is wrong? Describe (or draw) the situation, and write down the reason why practical help is most important.

The Buddha travelled around northern India for more than forty years teaching the Dharma. His followers became known as the Sangha, which means 'community'.

In Indian society at that time, people were divided into castes, rather like classes. A person was born into the same caste as his or her parents. If you were born into a high caste, you might become a doctor, a teacher or a priest. If you were a low caste, you had little chance to develop and improve yourself. Only the highest cast (the Brahmins) were allowed to teach from the scriptures and conduct religious ceremonies.

The Buddha did not agree with this. He mixed with people from all walks of life, accepted followers from any caste, and taught that all members of the Sangha were equal. All had the same chance of improving themselves by following the Noble Eightfold Path, no matter what their caste background.

Buddhists believe that it would be very difficult to follow the Dharma successfully on your own. This is how one modern Buddhist described it:

- The Sangha is like a community. You can't do it all on your own; you need friends to support and encourage you. That's what the Sangha is for.

Some of the Buddha's followers chose to give up their family life, and to travel around spreading his teaching. He organised them into communities of monks, known as **bhikkhus**. At first, most women continued to stay with their families; later communities were set up for nuns, who were called **bhikkhunis**.

They used to travel around the countryside teaching during the cooler and dryer months of the year. But when it was too hot or wet to do this, they gathered together in resting places (called **viharas**) to study the Dharma together.

As time went on, the viharas became permanent monasteries. Some monks lived in them all year, and they agreed on some other rules to help them organise their life together.

Those Buddhists who become monks or nuns take on a special responsibility for teaching the Dharma. But they are not priests. All Buddhists are responsible for the way in which they follow the teachings. Nobody else can do your own growing and developing for you; in the end it's up to you.

Most Buddhists do not choose to become monks or nuns. They follow the Buddha's teaching, and apply it to their work and family life. Nowadays the Sangha refers to *all* those who follow the Buddha, not just those who are monks or nuns.

In his 80th year the Buddha was taken ill, and died at Kushinara. He was cremated, and his ashes were distributed among the local kings in northern India where he had taught. They built memorials (called **stupas**) over the remains.

The most important places associated with the Buddha's life are Lumbini (where he was born), Bodh Gaya (where he became enlightened), Sarnath (where he preached his first sermon), and Kushinara, where he died. Some Buddhists try to visit these places, and walk round the stupas as a mark of respect.

▲ *This image shows Buddha on his deathbed*

1 Look at the illustrations on page 18. Write down at least two things that they tell you about the Buddhist Sangha.

2 Although they were sad to lose him, his followers were not surprised that the Buddha should grow old and die. Buddhists see death as a natural part of life.

a) Which teachings help them to understand death? (Look at page 12.)

b) Explain in your own words why they see death in this way.

3 Do you think it is a good idea to have memorials to people who have died? Write down your views.

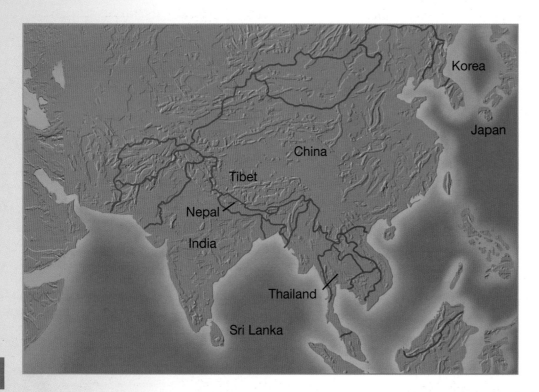

Today there are about 350 million Buddhists. Most of them live in the countries shown on this map, but others are found all over the world. There are thousands in Britain.

As Buddhism spread outwards from India, it gradually adapted to the needs of different peoples and cultures. As a result, there are several different kinds of Buddhism. In this chapter, we shall be looking at four of them – all of which are now found in Britain and in many other Western countries. This is how they started:

1 For the first two hundred years, Buddhism spread throughout India. Then, helped by the Buddhist Emperor Ashoka (273–232BCE), it was taken to Sri Lanka, Burma and Thailand. Buddhism in these countries is called Theravada Buddhism. This means 'the tradition of the **elders**'. It follows teaching handed down by senior monks from early times. **Monastic life** is very important in these countries. The monks wear yellow robes and are supported by the Buddhist householders.

2 After about five hundred years, Buddhism reached China, and then spread north to Korea and finally to Japan. In these countries religious people had usually been encouraged to marry and to work to support themselves and their families. Buddhism from these countries has fewer monks, and many of its teachers are married and have other work as well.

3 In the seventh century CE, Buddhism reached Tibet, where it developed very colourful forms of worship with music and chanting. Tibetan monks wear deep red robes. This form of Buddhism is found in Nepal, northern India, and throughout the Himalayan region.

4 At the beginning of the twentieth century Buddhism spread to the West. Today all three earlier kinds of Buddhism are practised in the West. Some Western Buddhist groups have developed the teachings in a way that they think is better for people in modern Western society.

Although they have different customs, dress and ways of worship, all three earlier branches of Buddhism follow the same basic teachings of the Buddha. Buddhists see them as different ways of following the same path towards enlightenment.

Monks, Nuns and Lay Buddhists

As the Buddha travelled around northern India, he came across three different kinds of people:

- Householders, who lived an ordinary family life, but who went to spiritual teachers such as himself for advice, and who gave food and money to support them.
- Monks and nuns, who often lived together in groups following particular teachers.
- Individuals who had retreated from society altogether, living alone in order to follow their religion. These were sometimes called 'forest dwellers'.

Most of the people who came to the Buddha were householders; he gave them teaching and they went back to their ordinary way of life, trying to put into practice what they had learned. But, as time went on, he gathered around himself groups of monks (and, later, nuns), who had 'gone forth' from family life. He also came across other groups of monks and nuns, followers of other teachers.

A Theravadin monk lives a very simple life, of **meditation**, study, teaching and work. He is allowed to have the following things:

- a simple yellow robe
- an offerings bowl
- a needle and cotton
- a string of beads (used to help concentration)
- a razor for shaving his head
- a net to strain drinking water (to remove insects).

The bowl is not for begging. The monks of Thailand do not beg for their food, but they go along to a village and wait to see if they will be given anything.

Householders come out and put food into the monks' bowls. They put their hands together and bow to the monks as a sign of respect. They thank the monks for receiving the offering, for giving them the opportunity to practise generosity, and for teaching the Buddhist path.

- When asked why he became a monk, Handa, a monk belonging to the Japanese Nipponsan Myohoji movement, said:

  'I was trying to discover who I really was. I was looking for something to which I could devote all my life.'

Because they do not have the many distractions and commitments of family and working life, monks and nuns can spend all their time practising and promoting the Dharma. Their life is disciplined, with time for meditation, study and work.

Of course, the majority of Buddhists are, and have always been, householders. They are called 'lay Buddhists'. But the Buddha's teachings were remembered and passed on among the groups of monks and nuns. They therefore had a very important part to play in continuing the Buddha's work, and in spreading his teaching.

---

1 Imagine that you have decided to become a Buddhist monk or nun. Write to a friend who is not a Buddhist, explaining why you have chosen this way of life.

2 Look at the list of the things that a Buddhist monk is allowed to have, then list the things that you need for happiness, and put them in order of importance. For example, would you start with a CD player? What do these things say about you?

● Theravada Buddhism

▲ *Monks receiving offerings of food in London. Giving in this way reminds the Buddhist community of the importance of the Buddha's teaching and of the fact that the lay and the monastic parts of the community are there to help one another*

The Theravada tradition of Buddhism follows a pattern of life and practice that goes back to the earliest days of the Sangha. Most followers of Theravada Buddhism would say that the life of a monk is the ideal way to follow the Buddha's teaching, freed from all distractions. On the other hand, they recognise that not everyone can become a monk or nun, so householders are content to help to support the monastic community, hoping that they will gain merit by doing this, and also benefiting from the teaching and advice given by the monks and nuns.

In some traditionally Buddhist countries, lay Buddhists look after the monks and nuns by giving them food and other things they need.

Feeding monks is also a sign of respect for the Buddha, his teachings and his followers. This lets the monks devote themselves to following and teaching the Buddhist path.

In return, the lay people believe that they benefit from the teaching. They also believe that they will become better Buddhists by practising generosity, and supporting monks is one way of doing this.

Theravadin monks generally wear saffron yellow robes. Early Buddhist monks probably wore this colour because saffron used to be a cheap dye, and the monks had no money. Other Buddhists wear different colours. The colour does not matter – what is important is the person's commitment to following the Buddhist path.

In this tradition, a boy may spend a short while in a monastery, living as a monk. This gives him a chance to learn more about his religion. It reminds him that he is a member of the Sangha, even though he may decide not to become a monk when he is older.

As a preparation for his spell as a monk, he has his head shaved. He is then given his robes and presented to the most senior monk of that particular vihara or monastery. After his monastic experience, he returns to his family, who may have a party to celebrate.

◄ *These Buddhist novices are being initiated in a special ceremony*

▲ *Although this temple is built in the same style as those in Thailand, it is in Wimbledon, South London*

Don't forget, although Theravada Buddhism is found chiefly in Sri Lanka and South East Asia, many Western Buddhists practise in this tradition. There are Theravadin temples, viharas and retreat centres (where people can go for a time of quiet, to learn meditation, or to study) throughout Britain. Some of those who attend are from South East Asia, and for them it is an important way of keeping in touch with the culture and life of their home countries, but many others are Westerners who have simply decided to take up this form of Buddhism.

1 Many young Theravada Buddhists spend a few weeks in a monastery to practise the discipline of the monastic life. List the advantages and disadvantages of trying out monastic life in this way.
2 Imagine you are a Buddhist. Explain to a non-Buddhist friend why you do not think that the monks are 'begging' when you give them offerings of food.

● Mahayana Buddhism

The form of Buddhism that spread north to China and then to Japan is called Mahayana Buddhism. The name means 'Great Vehicle' which suggests that it aims to help many people move along the Buddhist path, not just the few who are monks, or able to practise it full-time. There are many different forms of Mahayana Buddhism, over one hundred different ones in Japan alone. Many of these developed originally in China.

Three examples are Pure Land Buddhism, Nipponzan Myohoji and Zen.

PURE LAND BUDDHISM

Pure Land Buddhism is based on devotion to Amida Buddha. (His image is shown on page 32, where he sits in calm meditation.) Its followers chant Nembutsu. This is short for 'Namo Amida Butsu', meaning 'greeting Amida Buddha'. By doing this, they try to keep their minds aware of the Buddha. They believe that, by having faith in Amida Buddha, they will be released from the troubles of life into a pure 'Buddha land'. There, everything will be ideal for practising the Dharma.

Its religious leaders marry, eat meat, and work at ordinary jobs alongside their religious activities.

NIPPONZAN MYOHOJI

This is a modern Japanese Buddhist movement which is particularly concerned to promote peace. Its members have build Peace Pagodas all over the world.

Handa, a Japanese Buddhist monk living in England, explains why they have built the pagodas:

> ● By building peace pagodas, we express the Buddha's teaching that we should not kill. We should have respect for one another.

▲ *The Peace Pagoda in Battersea Park, London, was built by Nipponzan Myohoji, and there is another in Milton Keynes*

> ● When Buddhism arrived in China the people there were already following two religions, Confucianism and Taoism. The first emphasised respect for elders and family, the second encouraged people to live in a natural and harmonious way.
>
> As Buddhism became part of Chinese life, people accepted it alongside their other religions.

▲ *A Japanese Buddhist religious leader sits in meditation. His robes are quite different from those of the Theravadin or Tibetan monk*

24

● Zen

Meditation has always been an important part of Buddhism. We shall look at how Buddhists practise meditation on pages 42–45. In Japan there is a form of Buddhism called Zen that encourages the daily practice of meditation.

Meditation is a way of training your mind to see the truth about yourself and about life. It helps you become more aware of everything you do. Zen Buddhists (and others) believe that everyone has a Buddha nature within himself or herself. But most people don't recognise it or benefit from it. Training your mind helps you to develop that Buddha nature.

▲ *A Zen Buddhist Master during the tea-making ceremony*

Those who follow Zen Buddhism may take an ordinary activity (such as archery, making tea or arranging flowers) and become absorbed in every little detail of what is involved. What for most people would be a simple act of making tea, carried out without any particular thought, becomes, in Zen, a very delicate and beautiful thing, a way of calming and training the mind.

▲ *Part of a stone garden in Kyoto, Japan. The fine gravel is raked carefully to form patterns round the larger stones. Sitting quietly and looking at a garden like this might help a person to feel calm and peaceful*

Zen Buddhists believe that you cannot get far along the path to enlightenment *just* by thinking clearly. Nor do they think that you can achieve this simply by studying scriptures. Rather, the key thing is to be aware of all that is happening around you, to live in the present moment and give attention to your present action, rather than allowing your mind to go drifting off into memories of the past or dreams about the future. It is also important to allow your intuition to work, so that you have a natural sense of what is the right thing to do.

1 Which features of Indian Buddhism would it have been difficult for Chinese people to accept? How would you expect Buddhism to adapt itself to meet the needs of these people?

2 Look at the tea ceremony in the picture above. He will pour his tea slowly and thoughtfully.
   a) What are the differences between this and the way you might make a cup of tea?
   b) Do you pay careful attention when you make tea? Why do you think the person in the picture is so attentive?

3 Some problems are solved by thinking carefully. Others are solved by intuition – when you suddenly feel that something is right, even if you cannot explain why. Would logic or intuition be better for:
   a) working out a puzzle?
   b) choosing a colour to decorate a bedroom?
   c) becoming more aware of your thoughts and feelings?
   Explain your choices.

● Tibetan Buddhism

Tibetan Buddhism is very colourful. In temples and shrines you will see many different Buddha images, some very elaborate and strange, and there may be large wall-hangings called **thankas**.

During worship, **mantras** are chanted over and over. These are phrases which have a special symbolic meaning. There will be candles and lamps. At festivals, monks blow long horns, and there may be processions and dancing. People wearing costume act out Buddhist dramas.

All this is very different from what you find in Theravada or Zen Buddhism, where everything is kept simple. The reason for this is that Tibetan Buddhism encourages people to become involved in religion with their feelings and imagination as well as their thoughts.

Many of the features of Buddha images and worship that we shall be looking at later in this book come from the Tibetan tradition.

Tibetan Buddhists think of worship as something that goes on naturally all the time. They may chant mantras while going about their work. They also have machines to remind them of this continuous worship. Prayer wheels have prayers and mantras written inside them. Small ones, like the one shown here, are whirled round by hand. Larger ones may be set in a wall. As they turn, so the prayers inside them keep moving.

They also write prayers on pieces of cloth and hang them up as flags to blow in the wind. Tibetan Buddhists think of this as a way of joining in a kind of worship that goes on in nature all the time.

Study and debate are important features of life in Tibetan monasteries. The monks check that they have understood the teachings by debating them with one another.

▲ *The Tibetan New Year festival at the stupa at Boudhanath. Prayer flags have been put up and the monks recite prayers*

▲ *Young monks debating*

Young boys may spend some time in a monastery, living there and being educated by the monks. They go home to visit their parents from time to time. It is like a boarding school.

26

◄ *These Tibetan monks are chanting, as part of their worship. Although they are not in their usual shrine room, they have hung a thanka on the wall. They wear special headdresses*

The senior teachers in Tibetan Buddhism are called Lamas. The most famous is the Dalai Lama. You can see his picture on page 5. He was brought up in the Potala Palace in Lhasa, the capital of Tibet, and trained to be a spiritual leader.

In 1950, the Chinese invaded Tibet, which they considered to be part of China. The Dalai Lama escaped into India with many of his followers.

He represents the Buddhist people of Tibet, and argues that China should give Tibet its freedom again.

Because of the Chinese invasion, many Tibetan lamas have travelled to other parts of the world. As a result, Tibetan Buddhism is now far more widely known than it was before. Many Western Buddhists follow the Tibetan form of Buddhism.

● Choosing a teacher

Although you can start to learn about Buddhism from books, most Buddhists would say that you need an experienced teacher as a guide. Each individual needs to examine and apply Buddhist practice for himself or herself, and not everyone is ready for every part of the teaching.

Also, because they may be misunderstood, some teachings are kept secret, and only revealed to those whom their teacher believes to be ready for them.

1 a) People hang out flags on special occasions, and football fans wave rattles. Why do people do these things?

b) Write down why you think Tibetan Buddhists use prayer flags and wheels, and why they hang thankas from buildings at festival time.

2 Looking back over the last eight pages, make two lists, one to show the things that are special to Tibetan Buddhism, and the other to show those things that Tibetan Buddhism shares with other Buddhist traditions.

3 Which do you think is best – to learn about a religion from books, or to have a personal teacher to guide you? Give your reasons.

4 Try to find out more about the Dalai Lama, and the work he does for the people of Tibet.

Buddhism in the West

Buddhism is a universal religion. It can be practised by anyone, no matter where they come from. Describing the different forms of Buddhism as 'Tibetan' or 'Theravada' does not tell you about the people who follow it, only about where it originally came from. You don't have to be Tibetan to follow Tibetan Buddhism!

All of the main forms of Buddhism are taught and practised in Britain.

Some Buddhist places of worship are used by people from a particular country who have settled in Britain. The Thai Buddhist temple in South London is an example. The monks and people follow the same traditions of worship and dress as in Thailand, although they welcome other people to join them.

Other centres follow a particular Buddhist tradition which came originally from the East, but most of those who practise there have been born in Britain. For example Amaravati is a large monastery in Hertfordshire. It is one of four centres set up by the English Sangha Trust. It follows the traditions of the forest monasteries in Thailand, but that does not mean that its monks are Thai; many are British. Amaravati runs a retreat centre for those who want to spend some time in quiet reflection and study of the Dharma. People also visit the monastery to share in the worship or meditation, to take part in a festival or to hear a talk.

Other Western Buddhist groups have been set up in order to promote a particular Buddhist practice. The Samatha Trust, for example, teaches people how to practise samatha meditation, which helps to develop inner calm, strength of mind and clarity of thought.

People in the West often live busy lives. They may be worried about work or money. They may feel confused and anxious. Some may need help to relax and understand themselves better. Learning about meditation at a class may be the first step towards seeing what Buddhism has to offer.

◀ *A Tibetan centre in Britain*

● Buddhism and change

Remember two of the Buddha's most important teachings – that everything changes and that things happen as a result of the conditions that make them possible.

As Buddhism has spread, so it has changed. Tibetan and Japanese Buddhism look very different from the earlier Theravada tradition.

Buddhism in the West can never be exactly like that in the East, because its situation is different.

One of the new groups found in Britain is the 'Friends of the Western Buddhist Order' (FWBO). It uses the teaching and practices of all three of the Buddhist traditions, but it tries to adapt them to suit the needs of people in the West.

FWBO runs centres where people can come to learn about meditation and Buddhism. People who attend classes are called 'Friends'. Most of its centres are simply named after where they are found, for example 'The London Buddhist Centre' or 'The Manchester Buddhist Centre'.

Some of the teachings and practices of the FWBO are very different from those found in the rest of the Buddhist world, which has led some people to question whether they should be thought of as Buddhist at all. However, those who belong to the FWBO certainly think of themselves as Buddhist, and many of their basic teachings are the same as in other Buddhist groups.

▲ This is a yoga class run at a Buddhist centre. You do not have to be a Buddhist to benefit from this

Members of the Western Buddhist Order itself are not monks or nuns. The FWBO encourages people to think about living in single-sex communities, and some married couples choose to live separately in this way. Others, however, continue to live on their own, or in families.

This is very different from the usual Buddhist way, which is for people to live a normal family life unless they choose to become a monk or a nun for a period of time. (In Buddhism, monks and nuns do not take vows for life, but can choose from time to time whether to continue in the monastic life or return to being a householder.)

29

▲ This restaurant is run by a team of Buddhists. It is a 'right livelihood' business (see step 5 of the Noble Eightfold Path on page 14) because it is run on Buddhist principles. Many of those who join the FWBO give up their jobs and careers in order to work in businesses like this

In the rest of this book we shall be looking at many different features of Buddhist teachings and practices. Having seen the different kinds of Buddhism in this chapter, you will realise that not every Buddhist you meet will practise everything that you read about here. Some emphasise one thing and some another.

One thing all the different kinds of Buddhism have in common is that they are based on the Buddha, his teaching and the community of his followers.

1 a) Think about the life you lead now and how you expect to live when you are older. Perhaps you may be married with children. Make a list of the things you expect to be important in your life.
b) Then think about what you have learnt so far about Buddhism. What features of life in the West make it difficult for someone to practise Buddhism? What features of Buddhism make it especially useful for Westerners?
c) In what ways do you think Buddhism might change as more Western people start to follow it?

A refuge is a place of shelter and security. Most people go to some sort of refuge in their quest for happiness. Some go for refuge to their best friend, and feel miserable without him or her. Others go for refuge to the work they do, or to their hobbies or interests. Some go for refuge to money; some want power or fame. When you have your refuge you feel secure; without it, you may feel quite lost.

Buddhists think that it is a bad idea to go for refuge to money or to work or to another person. All of these things can change and let you down. None of them can save you from suffering.

Buddhists 'go for refuge' to the Buddha, his teaching and the community of his followers.

Going for refuge in this way is not an attempt to run away from life and its problems. Buddhists see it as going for refuge *to* life, for they always try to understand the truth about life. It is those who go for refuge to money or to other limited things, who are really trying to run away.

The usual way to show that you are determined to put the Buddha's teaching into practice is by saying the '**Refuges and Precepts**' in front of one or more ordained members of the Buddhist community. The 'precepts' are five guidelines on how to live as a Buddhist (they are in Chapter 13).

A person repeats three times:

> I go to the Buddha for refuge.
> I go to the Dharma for refuge.
> I go to the Sangha for refuge.

People need to know something about Buddhist teaching before they can decide to go for refuge. But they are not expected to understand everything beforehand.

Buddhists understand that they will spend the rest of their lives learning about the Dharma, and how to practise it. Going for refuge means that they have chosen to start out on the Buddhist path.

When a person 'takes the refuges and precepts' at a shrine, he or she will usually make three simple offerings – a candle, a flower and a stick of incense.

The candle represents the light of wisdom, shining to illuminate the path through life.

▲ *Here are some things to which people might go for refuge*

The flower is beautiful, but very soon it will fade and die. It represents the idea that everything in life will eventually change; we cannot stop that happening, any more than we can stop a beautiful flower from fading.

◄ *Going for refuge is not something that a person does just once. Buddhists regularly need to think about what it means for them. These Buddhists meet together as a group to discuss their commitment to the Buddhist way of life*

The smell of incense spreads out to fill a room. This is a reminder that good deeds spread outwards from the person who performs them. They have an effect on the whole world.

These offerings are not special to the ceremony when someone 'goes for refuge'. They can be made at other times as well.

When a person has gone for refuge as a Buddhist, he or she will try:

- to follow the example of the Buddha
- to improve his or her understanding of the Buddha's teaching
- to test out that teaching in practical ways and to apply it to his or her life
- to practise meditation
- to support others who are following the same path.

Alan has been a Buddhist for many years. This is how he described why he went for refuge:

- Most things, like hobbies, are limited. But Buddhism is so huge. You can put your whole life into it. You know that everything you do will be worthwhile. There's the feeling that ultimately you can't fail; you are going to benefit.

This may sound difficult, but Buddhists see it as a chance to achieve something worthwhile, both for themselves and for others.

Although Buddhists may hope to benefit by feeling inner peace and happiness, they do not think this is selfish. By developing friendship and **compassion**, they seek to help all other creatures as well.

1 **a)** Write down in your own words what it means to 'go for refuge'.

b) Why do people go for refuge to something, whether they are religious or not?

2 **a)** Make a list of at least six things to which people might go for refuge. Against each of these, write what a person might hope to gain by going for refuge to that thing.

b) Write down any problems with each refuge. (Clue: why might it let them down?)

3 **a)** Look back at pages 6–9. List the things to which Siddhartha might have gone for refuge.

b) Explain why you think he rejected them.

4 **a)** Why do you think some people like to have a ceremony when they join a religion?

b) Do you think it makes any difference to the way they try to follow that religion? Explain your answer.

▲ *Amitabha (or Amida) Buddha, in a position of meditation*

they have seen. These are the many Buddhas and **Bodhisattvas** (enlightened beings to whom Buddhists may look for guidance and inspiration) that you see in shrines. Each represents one special aspect of enlightenment.

▲ *This is a modern Western image of the Buddha*

In Buddhist shrines you may find many different Buddha images. Some are male and some female, some look kindly and some are fierce; some have very simple costumes while others are dressed like princes with royal headdresses. Some are brightly coloured, and some have many arms or heads. Only a few may actually resemble your idea of the historical Buddha. Who are all these Buddhas?

Some images *do* represent the historical Buddha. He may be shown teaching, or sitting in meditation. Some images show him lying on his side.

Other images are quite different. They show different aspects of enlightenment – aspects of what it would be like to be a Buddha. These include showing compassion, and putting your energy into doing good, being calm in meditation, and developing skill in teaching.

Buddhists have meditated on all these qualities. As a result they have created images to show what

Buddhists often have a number of different Buddha images at home. The images inspire Buddhists with the particular qualities that they want to develop in themselves. Buddhists may have one or two favourite images. Some prefer to have only images of the historical Buddha, Shakyamuni.

● I have three Buddha images and some photographs set out on a shelf where I meditate.

I prefer the simple images of Shakyamuni. But I like others as well. Some are very elaborate. To me they represent Buddhahood in a kind of ideal realm. An image of Avalokiteshvara, for example, represents compassion in a pure form.

32

▲ *This is an image of the Bodhisattva Manjugosha. The sword represents wisdom. He cuts through ignorance with it*

Some of these images show beautiful young men and women, dressed as princes and princesses. These images represent the inner experiences of spiritual wealth and happiness.

As you look at the various images shown in this chapter, remember that they do not pretend to give you an idea of what the historical Buddha looked like. They are meant to get your imagination going. You should not ask 'Is this image right or wrong?' but 'What is this image trying to tell me about Buddhism? Or about myself?'

Images can be very powerful. They can help us to choose what we do with our life. They can persuade us to buy one thing rather than another. They can shape the way in which a country is governed, by promoting a political party, for example.

Here is an example of an image that is designed to influence you:

You won't become more handsome or beautiful simply by buying a particular product. But the advertisement suggests that this is the sort of person who would buy it – and if you want to be like them, you had better buy it too!

You know it isn't literally true, but it works just the same.

---

1 a) Draw four different images of yourself. Let each image show one particular thing about you, or one activity in which you like to take part. If you colour the images, think carefully about what colours to use. Let each colour express your feelings about that part of yourself.

b) Label each of them, 'This is me when . . .'.

c) Write down which of the images is your favourite, and say why. (You now have a set of images of yourself, just like the different Buddha images.)

2 Buddha images are dressed (e.g. like a prince or a monk) to show the feelings or qualities of that image. Write down some ways in which you dress to express your personality.

Some Buddha images, found mainly in the Tibetan tradition, seem to be bursting with energy. They may express anger and determination, like this one:

▲ *A **wrathful** Buddha image*

This is how one Buddhist described the use of wrathful images:

- Anger can be destructive, as when a small child loses its temper and hits out in all directions. But the energy that causes anger can be used in a positive way, removing obstacles in life and getting things done. In wrathful images, I see a burst of energy that can overcome difficulties.

Remember, Buddhism is a method of training the mind. But you can't do that until you learn to look at all aspects of yourself, including emotions like love and hate. Buddhists believe that you should be aware of the arising of each of these emotions. In other words, as you experience anger, you need to become aware of exactly why it is you are angry. Then the next step is to learn how to use all the energy that is bottled up in your anger in a positive way. One of the qualities of the Buddhist life is energy directed at doing good. So the wrathful image is a reminder that we can use our anger to do something positive to improve our situation.

The Buddhist life is sometimes summed up in two words: wisdom and compassion. These express the two sides of Buddhism. On the one hand there is the quiet understanding of the truth about life, and on the other there are the precepts which aim to guide people into a way of life that shows compassion towards all living things. In the image of the Buddha, these two things come together. This is expressed in images which show a sexual couple. These are not meant to be about sex itself, but express the joining of wisdom (represented by the female) and compassion (represented by the male).

▲ *A Yab-Yum (mother-father) image does not represent physical sex. It expresses the joining of wisdom and compassion*

Some Western people think that it is strange to have sexual images in a religion, and may even feel embarrassed by them, but in traditional Buddhist societies thay are treated with very great respect.

Don't forget: these are images. Buddhists do not think that these Buddhas and Bodhisattvas exist in the ordinary world of space and time. You will never see a Bodhisattva through a telescope!

But in meditation and worship, Buddhists feel that these beings are very real. They inspire them, and help them to understand their own anger, wisdom or compassion.

They try to show something of what enlightenment is like, and in that way they help people to move closer to enlightenment themselves.

Some things to look for in a Buddha image

You can learn a lot about what an image is trying to show from the position of the hands. These hand positions are called 'mudras', and each mudra has a special meaning.

Some images are very simple, while others are elaborate. Most of them include some symbols which tell us things about the Buddhist path. Here are some of the symbols and what they mean:

Images of the historical Buddha often have a flame coming out of the top of his head. This is to show that he is enlightened.

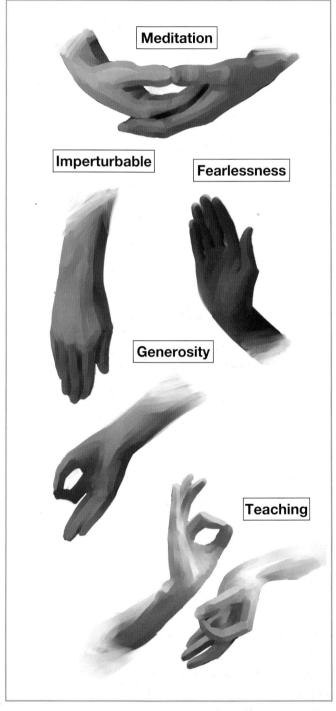

Meditation

Imperturbable

Fearlessness

Generosity

Teaching

▲ *If a person is 'imperturbable', it means that he or she cannot be distracted from doing what is right. Siddhartha was determined to become enlightened as he sat under the Bo-tree, so he is shown there with this mudra (see page 10)*

In ancient India there were lists of features that were traditionally believed to be found on a holy man. Naturally, the first images of the Buddha showed these marks. The most immediately noticeable of these are the long earlobes.

● The Buddha can be anyone

Buddha images do not necessarily represent the historical Buddha, Siddhartha Gautama. Everyone has the potential to become a Buddha, and therefore the Buddha's image can be anyone's image. In India, most of the images are Indian, in China, his features are Chinese, and in the West many new Buddha images have Western features. There are also female Buddhas.

1 Imagine you are with a group of people walking around an exhibition of Buddhist art and you come across some Tibetan Yab-Yum images. Some of those with you snigger, and say that it's weird to have sexual images in religion. Write down how you would explain that the images are not really about sex, and why they are treated with such respect by Buddhists.

2 **a)** Invent your own set of mudras. Working in pairs, draw them and then get your partner to guess what they mean. Your partner might want to suggest improvements to make the meaning clearer.

   b) Write down your explanation against each of them.

▲ Here are two very different images of Avalokiteshvara. One shows him stepping down, the other shows him with a thousand arms. Although the images look different, their meaning is very similar

A popular image is that of the Bodhisattva of Compassion (Avalokiteshvara). He is sometimes shown with a thousand arms, radiating out from him like the spokes of a wheel. That means that he is ready to help anywhere and in any situation.

Some images have movement in them. Stepping down from his throne indicates that this bodhisattva wants to come and help people – another way of expressing his compassion.

Some Buddhas hold a vajra. The word vajra can mean two things – a diamond, or a thunderbolt. The vajra can represent something hard, determined and unbreakable (like the diamond) and also something sudden and powerful (like the thunderbolt). The vajra represents all that is powerful and determined about the Buddhist path.

▼ A vajra

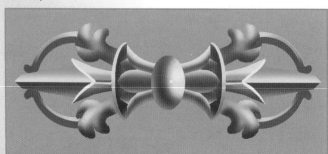

▲ In China the Bodhisattva of Compassion is shown in female form. She is called Kwan-shih-yin, or Kwan-yin

Sometimes a Buddha may hold a lotus blossom, or sit on a throne made up of a lotus with its petals opening outwards. For Buddhists, the lotus flower is an image of enlightenment. A lotus takes its nourishment from the mud, grows up through the deep water, and finally opens beautifully into the sunlight. Buddhists use this to illustrate the path that the human mind can take, from the mud of anger, greed and ignorance up to the clear air of enlightenment.

A lotus closes up tight, and then gradually opens its petals. This is like the mind opening up to wisdom, love and compassion.

▲ Buddha's footprint at Bodh Gaya

▲ An eight-spoked wheel. Why do you think the Buddha was represented in this way? Clue: think about his teachings

In the first centuries after the Buddha's death, there were no Buddha images of the sort that we have seen in this chapter. Instead, his followers represented him in a number of other ways: through a stupa (a monument in which the cremated remains of someone are kept), a eight-spoked wheel, or even a footprint.

1 Do you have any posters of musicians or film stars in your room? Why? What do you think about when you look at them? What do they say about you?
2 Finish off the following sentence. 'Buddhists find images helpful because . . .'
3 Look at the two images of Avalokiteshvara shown on the opposite page. Write down the way in which each of them illustrates that he is the Bodhisattva of *Compassion*.
4 **a)** Look carefully at the other Buddhist images shown in this chapter and choose the two that you find most interesting.
   b) Write down the name (or the description) of each of your chosen images. Then, next to it, write down the sort of feelings that the image suggests to you.
   c) Then write down what each of them tells you about the Buddhist path.
5 Do you think it would be more helpful to have just one single image of the Buddha, rather than this great variety? Give reasons for your answer.

Buddhist worship is called **puja**. It takes place at a shrine, and may include:

- chanting
- making offerings in front of a Buddha image
- listening to readings from **scriptures**
- reciting short passages together.

Worship is a way of showing respect and gratitude to the Buddha for his inspiration and his teaching. It is something to feel and enjoy. Puja is a way of sharing and celebrating together.

Buddhism is not just a set of ideas; it is a whole way of life. Buddhists can show this in a puja by expressing their devotion to the Buddha, and in their lives by everything they do.

In most places where Buddhists meet together you will find a room for worship and meditation. It contains an image or images of the Buddha, and room for people to sit on the floor. It is called a shrine room. Any place where a Buddha image is used in worship is also called a shrine. Buddhists may have a shrine at home, too.

Here are some things you may find at a shrine:

- *Buddha images* – you may find many different Buddha images on a shrine. This is because there are different ways of representing enlightenment. They are called **rupas**.
- *Offering bowls* – offerings are made as though the Buddha himself were present as an honoured guest. A visitor, arriving after a journey, might be given water to wash with, perfume, or different kinds of food and drink. On a shrine, these offerings are usually represented by seven bowls of water, set out in front of an image of the Buddha.
- *Flowers, candles and incense* – these are the three traditional offerings that Buddhists make at a shrine.

You may see other things in the shrine room:

- *Cushions* for people to sit on when they meditate. These may be set out in long rows, facing each other across the shrine room.
- *A small bell or gong.* This is used to tell people when it is time to start the next step in a meditation or puja.

38

▶ *The shrine in the Croydon Buddhist Centre, South London*

By repeating the mantra, Buddhists allow the compassionate aspect of enlightenment to break through into their minds.

- You don't have to know the meaning in a word-for-word sense – but you just have to know what the mantra represents.

▲ *Offering incense at a shrine*

- According to Buddhism, we practise on three levels – body, speech and mind. I think puja is important because it involves all of these. You can put the whole of yourself into a puja.

As part of their worship, Buddhists may chant mantras. These are phrases in Sanskrit (the ancient Indian religious language). Often, they do not have any straightforward meaning. You cannot simply translate a mantra into English.

Mantras are 'sound symbols'. A mantra combines special sounds to express some particular aspect of enlightenment. Each mantra is associated with one of the Buddha images.

One of the best known mantras is:

OM MANI PADME HUM

This is the mantra of Avalokiteshvara, the Bodhisattva of Compassion. It expresses love and compassion for all.

OM – this is an ancient Indian sound. For Buddhists it represents the goal at which they are aiming.
MANI – this means 'treasure or jewel'.
PADME – this means 'lotus'.
HUM – this is a special syllable that represents Avalokiteshvara.

The Buddha, Dharma and Sangha are sometimes called 'jewels'. The lotus represents the human mind opening up to enlightenment.

Avalokiteshvara is sometimes called 'the jewel in the lotus'.

▲ *Beautifully embroidered images of Buddhas and Bodhisattvas are often hung on the walls of shrine rooms. These are called thankas*

1 a) Copy and complete this grid, using the clues below.

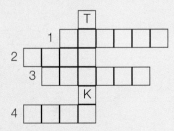

1 A place where you find an image of the Buddha.
2 A Buddha image.
3 Buddhists chant this.
4 Buddhist worship.
b) Copy out the word that goes down, and give its meaning.
2 Write down any words from a pop song which (like those in some mantras) do not make sense, but are still part of the song.

● Different kinds of temples and shrines

There are many different kinds of places to which Buddhists may go to meditate, to make an offering or to join in puja.

The simplest of these are **monuments** believed to contain **relics** of the Buddha. In India they are called stupas, and in Sri Lanka dagobas. They are solid, dome-shaped buildings. They may be small or large. Buddhists walk round stupas as a sign of respect. These monuments are often found in monasteries, and at places of pilgrimage. In Thailand they are are often bell-shaped and beautifully decorated. They, and the worship areas and monasteries that surround them, are called wats. In Burma they are called pagodas, and Tibetan Buddhists call them chortens. Around them are shrines, at which people make offerings.

As well as these monuments, there are temples which have rooms for people to gather together to meditate or chant, and where they can pay their respect to the Buddha by making offerings before Buddha images.

There is no general rule about how often a Buddhist should visit a temple. Some will do so regularly. Others go only at festivals or when they feel they need to.

▲ In front of this chorten you can see the shrines where offerings can be made and a row of prayer wheels to be turned by hand

▲ Inside a temple in Thailand. Can you see the monks cleaning the statue?

When taking part in worship, Buddhists sometimes put their cupped hands together. This may represent a lotus flower.

Some Buddhists bow deeply or even lie on the ground in front of an image. It is a sign that they owe everything they have to the Buddha and his teachings. They are bowing to the Buddha himself – *not* just to the image in front of them. Buddhists do not worship Buddha images themselves. They treat them with the same respect that they would show to the Buddha if he were present.

▲ *On this shrine the image is of the Buddha teaching (see the mudras on page 35)*

Buddhists may also have small shrines in their homes – perhaps a Buddha image, with some flowers, or an incense stick burning. This will often be in a quiet place where they sit to meditate.

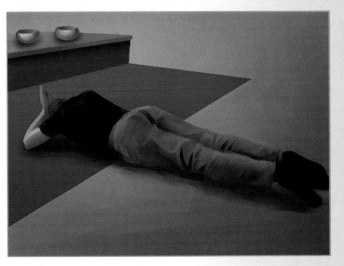

On entering a shrine room, Buddhists normally turn to face the shrine, put their hands together and bow to the Buddha image as a sign of their devotion.

1 Imagine you are a Buddhist. Write to a non-Buddhist friend, explaining why you bow or lie down in front of statues of the Buddha.
2 Do you think it is best to go to a place of worship regularly, or only when you feel the need to? Give reasons for your answer.
3 Some shrines are quite simple, perhaps with just a Buddha image and some candles and incense burning. Others are very elaborate. Which do you feel is the more useful for following the Buddhist path? Give your reasons.

If you read something that interests you, the time passes quickly, you feel relaxed but alert and you remember what you read. Your mind is focussed on a single point of interest. But if you try to learn something that you find boring, time passes slowly, you feel tired and you can't remember it without making an effort. Your mind pulls you in many different directions and you achieve little.

Buddhists say that the same thing applies to life. In order to live life to the full, you need to calm and train your mind. This helps you to be more aware of yourself and those around you. The means of doing this is meditation.

There are two kinds of meditation – Samatha and Vipassana meditation.

● Samatha meditation

This helps the mind to become calm, so that it is alert and gently focussed on a simple object or idea.

One way of doing this is to become aware of your breathing – feeling the air gently fill your lungs and then flow out through your nostrils. This brings calmness and a greater awareness of yourself and your physical body.

This is how one Buddhist described it:

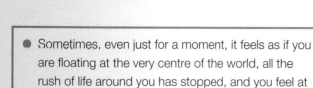
> ● Sometimes, even just for a moment, it feels as if you are floating at the very centre of the world, all the rush of life around you has stopped, and you feel at home in yourself.

As you go deeper in meditation, you reach different levels. They can be described by images:
● being filled with joy, like soap powder which is completely dissolved in a bowl of water
● fresh water bubbling up from a spring at the bottom of a pool
● lotus flowers growing up through the fresh water towards the light above
● being wrapped round in a white cloak.

This is what meditation can feel like.

The best way to judge meditation is not by what happens while you are meditating, but what happens afterwards. If meditation is working well, you should gradually start to become calmer and more contented in your ordinary life, less likely to get irritable or unreasonable.

▲ *A Western Buddhist meditating at a shrine in Thailand*

42

▲ *These monks in India are making a mandala (pattern of images with spiritual meaning) out of coloured sand. They take great care over every little detail, but when the mandala is finished it will be thrown away. Buddhists believe that things can be precious or created with great care, but that does not mean we have to cling on to them*

If you give attention to any activity, however simple, your mind will become focussed and calm. Sometimes this can take the form of working on a design. Look at the attention the monks are giving to the sand mandala in the photo above. What is important is not the end result, but the way in which the work is done.

There are many examples of meditation through action in the Zen tradition of Buddhism. Whether it is in archery or painting, flower arranging or raking the elaborate patterns in a sand garden, all sorts of actions give opportunities for calm meditation.

1 Have you ever become so engrossed in what you are doing that you have completely forgotten where you are or what time of day it is? Have you ever concentrated on something so closely that every other thought has left your mind? If so, try to write down how it felt while you were having that experience, and how you felt afterwards when you 'came out of' that very concentrated state.

2 Here is an exercise to see how still your mind can become, or how easily you can be distracted: Breathe in and out. Concentrate on being aware of the breath going in and out of your body. Then silently count 'one'. Take another breath and count 'two'.

Try to continue concentrating on your breath. If your mind wanders, start again at 'one'. Try to continue like this until you reach a count of ten. Then write down how you felt while doing this, and if you found it easy or hard.

3 We can sometimes be very possessive of things that we have made, especially if we have taken a lot of trouble over them. We may become angry if anyone criticises them or mistreats them in some way. Imagine you are a Tibetan Buddhist. You have just finished making a sand mandala. A non-Buddhist says he or she thinks you have wasted your time, because the image will be thrown away. How would you reply?

● Vipassana meditation

This is 'insight' meditation. Buddhists say that it helps them to see the truth about life. It can involve taking an aspect of Buddhist teaching and holding an image of it in your mind.

For example, some Buddhists meditate on flowers. They see that they are beautiful now, but they will quickly fade and die. They call to mind that all life involves changes of that sort. We can enjoy beautiful things, but we know that they cannot last for ever.

Some Buddhists meditate on death. They might imagine a corpse about to be cremated. We will all die one day, and Buddhists say that it is something we should keep in mind when we think about life.

People who have narrowly escaped death sometimes say that nothing can ever really worry them after that. Vipassana meditation is a bit like that. Once you are aware of the fact that one day you are going to die, then it is easier to show compassion to others without always worrying about yourself.

▲ *A Zen meditation hall*

Zen Buddhists have meditation halls, where they sit in rows to meditate. These are often very plain and simple buildings. This reflects the simplicity and calmness that is the goal of meditation.

The monks sit facing a blank wall, so that they see nothing to distract them. Another monk walks up and down behind them with a flat wooden rod. He keeps watch over those who are meditating. If someone appears to be getting drowsy, he gives them a sharp tap with the rod.

● Chanting

Some Buddhists, particularly in the Japanese Nichiren traditions, practise chanting rather than meditation. They take a simple phrase and chant it over and over. These phrases are called mantras, and they are also used in Tibetan and other forms of Buddhism.

The effect of chanting a mantra can be similar to that of other forms of meditation, as you become actively calm and totally concentrated in what you are chanting.

Buddhists normally try this kind of meditation only with the guidance of an experienced Buddhist teacher. Vipassana meditation is serious business, and – like a medicine – it can do more harm than good if taken wrongly.

That does not mean there is anything wrong with them, only that they can be harmful if misused. Many of the more serious meditation practices therefore come 'on prescription only'.

In order to help their meditation, Buddhists may visualise a particular Buddha image. They hold it and what it represents in their mind. Sometimes they imagine themselves becoming that Buddha image. For example, they feel what it is like to have the compassion of the Bodhisattva Avalokiteshvara.

Right mindfulness – being aware of yourself and of others – is one of the steps on the Noble Eightfold Path. Buddhists believe that the practice of meditation is one of the best ways to become mindful.

But meditation is not an end in itself; it is a means of developing qualities of calmness, insight and compassion. The benefits of meditation are shown in the way people live and the friendliness and kindness that they show.

How do you know if meditation is doing you any good? This is what one Buddhist has to say:

● I don't look for an end result after each session. Meditation is a long-term process. It's a regular habit through which you hope to develop. On the other hand, you hope that each time you meditate you will become a bit more aware of what's going on around you. So if you have a good session, you get benefits straight away.

This is the usual way in which people make progress with their meditation. But sometimes they may suddenly see things in a new way.

● Developing Loving-Kindness

Sometimes meditation aims to develop a particular emotion – for example, **metta** (loving-kindness).

To do this, you first calm yourself and then gradually bring people to mind, including a good friend and someone you find it difficult to get on with. As you imagine that person you cultivate warm, friendly feelings towards them.

Gradually, as the meditation goes on, you may extend these friendly emotions outwards, so that you feel goodwill to those who live around you, and then out further to include *all* creatures.

1 Look at the illustrations and passage from the Dhammapada on page 16. Think about this passage, and then write down why you think a Buddhist might say that meditation can have an important influence on what we do in our ordinary lives.

2 Do you think that there are some things – like death – that are so terrible that people should not meditate on them? What do you think a Buddhist would have to say about this?

▲ *Buddhists in Thailand celebrate the new year by showing compassion to all living things. This Thai girl is releasing an eel into the river to gain merit*

There are no fixed rules about how Buddhists should celebrate festivals. The Buddha taught that people should not trust religious ceremonies for their own sake. For a Buddhist, it is not the ceremony itself that is important. What matters is the attitude of mind of those who take part in it.

So Buddhists are less concerned about what they should do at festivals than about following the Buddha and his teaching.

Buddhists do not think that they will gain any benefit simply by attending a festival. The value of a festival is that it gives Buddhists the opportunity to celebrate together in an atmosphere of friendliness and understanding. It is also a chance to learn more about the teachings of the Buddha.

A most important festival for Buddhists is **Wesak**. This is celebrated at the time of the full moon in May. It recalls the birth, enlightenment and death of the Buddha. There may be processions, with shrines specially decorated for the festival. In some places, it is customary to decorate the home with candles at Wesak.

In some countries there is a New Year festival. In Thailand it takes place in April and is called Songkran Day. Water is an important symbol for cleaning, refreshment and new life. On Songkran Day, people wash Buddha images and splash one another with water. They also rescue fish from dried-up rivers and put them into fresh water, and release birds from cages.

▶ *These Thai youngsters celebrate New Year with a water fight*

Almost every month, the day of the full moon is celebrated as a festival in some traditional Buddhist countries. In July, many Buddhists celebrate the time when the Buddha started to teach the Dharma.

Buddhists also have festivals to remember other famous teachers, like Padmasambhava, who brought Buddhism to Tibet.

In the early days of Buddhism, each autumn, during the rainy season, the monks used to gather together and study, because the weather stopped them going out to teach. In many places, monks still gather for a retreat in the autumn. This is a time when some people like to make offerings to them. They give practical things, like material for robes, to help them with their work. This 'festival of giving' is called the Kathina.

Sometimes they make large images out of butter. These gradually melt and lose their beauty. This is a reminder that even the most beautiful things are going to change and die. They may also produce mandalas out of sand. Even though these may eventually be thrown away, Buddhists still take great care over making them. It is important to be able to create something, to love it, and then to let it go. (There is a photo of a mandala being created on page 43.)

▲ At the Kathina ceremony, monks are given gifts. These Theravadin monks from Wimbledon sit behind their offering bowls while people pass down the row giving something to each of them

Tibetan Buddhists celebrate festivals with dancing and drama. They may wear elaborate costumes for this. They take part in processions, and blow horns.

▲ Like the sand mandalas, butter images are created in the knowledge that they won't last

---

1 a) Write down some of the traditional ways in which Buddhists celebrate Songkran Day in Thailand.
   b) Say what feelings you think a Buddhist might have when he or she takes part in this festival.
   c) Do a drawing to illustrate Songkran Day.

2 List some reasons why you think it might be useful to have special days for celebration.

3 List the Buddhist teachings that are illustrated by the festival activities described in this chapter.

Buddhism does not set down rules which everyone must obey all the time out of fear of being punished. There are two reasons for this:

1. There is no god in Buddhism to reward or punish people, or to set down laws.
2. No two people are the same, you need to judge what is right in your own circumstances, not simply obey rules.

But, of course, Buddhists believe that you have to live with the consequences of what you do.

Instead of rules, Buddhism gives precepts (guidelines). These help people to avoid actions which are likely to bring about harmful results, for themselves and others.

● The Five Precepts

There are five precepts that all Buddhists try to follow:

1 I WILL AVOID TAKING LIFE

- that means not killing people

- animals too? Many Buddhists are vegetarian

- and the Earth! It means not destroying the natural world around us

The positive side of this precept is:
I will try to show loving-kindness towards all creatures.

2 I WILL AVOID TAKING WHAT IS NOT GIVEN

- not stealing

- not trying to get more than my fair share

- not trying to grab at wealth or power or fame at the expense of others

The positive side of this precept is:
I will try to be generous and willing to share.

3 I WILL AVOID HARMFUL SEXUAL ACTIVITY

- not hurting other people through sex

The positive side of this precept is:
I will act responsibly.

Although this third precept is usually applied to sexual activity, it is really about misuse of all the senses. In other words, it is about not grabbing at things to satisfy your own wants all the time. So people who eat and drink too much, or want to spend all their time shopping for new clothes, could be said to be going against this precept.

4 I WILL AVOID SAYING WHAT IS NOT TRUE

- not deliberately lying

- not trying to give the wrong impression

- not even being dishonest with yourself

The positive side of this precept is:
I will try to be completely truthful – honest and open in everything I say.

5 I WILL AVOID CLOUDING MY MIND WITH ALCOHOL OR DRUGS

- not getting drunk

- not doing anything that clouds your mind and takes you over. This might include things like gambling, or being hooked on arcade games

The positive side of this precept is:
I will try to keep my mind clear, so that I can be alert and aware of everything around me.

This last precept is specially important. Buddhism is all about being aware of the world around you and how you respond to it. It is about being aware of those things that cause suffering and unhappiness, and learning how to overcome them.

We can't do that if we try to escape from reality into a world of our own.

● Rules for Monks and Nuns

The Precepts are general principles by which all Buddhists try to live. They are not fixed rules, but give an idea of what the best sort of life would be for someone who wants to avoid causing suffering and make progress along the Buddhist path.

Those who become monks or nuns, however, accept many detailed rules about how they should live. These are necessary, if they are to live together happily.

They lead a very **disciplined** life, generally eating only before midday, and accepting only the very basic necessities of life.

They choose to accept these rules in order to be able to concentrate on their chosen way of life, and know that they will not offend, or be offended by, the other people with whom they live.

If they do not keep the most important of these rules, they may even be asked to leave the monastic life and become lay Buddhists again.

Some lay Buddhists accept extra rules for a short time – perhaps during a festival – as a voluntary act of self-discipline.

1 Which do you think is easier, obeying a rule or trying to follow a precept? Give your reasons.
2 If you are unable to keep the fifth precept, you are unlikely to make progress in keeping the others. Why?
3 Keeping the precepts is a way to avoid causing suffering to others as well as yourself. Write down examples of how breaking each of the precepts can

cause suffering. In groups, act out role plays to illustrate each of them.
4 Think about what is involved with keeping the five precepts, and then write down a description of a way of life that reflects all the positive things that the precepts encourage.

Buddhists freely choose to follow the five precepts. They are not absolute rules. For example, if a person needs to eat meat in order to keep healthy, then he or she may do so. After all, if you end up harming yourself in the attempt not to harm other creatures, you have still gone against the first precept! Buddhists have to make up their own minds about how best to follow the precepts, although they may receive guidance from their teachers.

Buddhists point out that a person who acts foolishly will eventually suffer the consequences, and will spoil the very things that make life worthwhile.

> ● He who destroys life, who utters lies, who takes what is not given to him, who goes with the wife of another, who gets drunk with strong drinks – he digs up the very roots of his life.
>
> *Dhammapada 246*

Following the precepts is a job for life. Buddhists do not expect to succeed all at once:

> ● Let a wise man remove impurities from himself even as a silversmith removes impurities from the silver: one after another, little by little, again and again.
>
> *Dhammapada 239*

Buddhists try to develop four personal qualities. They form the basis of the Buddhist way of life. They are like lights to guide a person through life.

Love • Compassion • Joy • Peace

Buddhists describe actions as either unskilful or skilful. They are unskilful if they are foolish and likely to lead to more ignorance, anger and greed. They are skilful if they are the result of wise choices, and are likely to lead people towards peace and happiness.

● A Zen Story

Two Japanese monks, Tanzan and Ekido, were walking along the road. It was a wet day and the road was very muddy.

Coming round a bend, they saw a beautiful girl in a silk kimono and sash, standing on the side unable to cross the mud.

Although he was a monk, Tanzan walked straight up to the girl.

'Come on,' he said.

Lifting her up in his arms he carried her over the mud and set her down on the other side.

Then they walked on.

Ekido said nothing for a long time, but when they reached the temple where they were to stay, he could contain himself no longer.

'We monks should not go near females,' he protested. 'Especially not young and beautiful ones! It is dangerous! Why did you pick her up and carry her like that?'

'I left the girl there on the side of the road,' Tanzan replied. 'Are you still carrying her?'

Right Livelihood

A Buddhist who seriously tries to live according to the five precepts will think carefully about the sort of work that he or she will do. Buddhists who run businesses need to think about how their Buddhist precepts affect the way in which they treat their customers and fellow employees.

> • As the bee takes the essence of a flower and flies away without destroying its beauty and perfume, so let the sage wander in this life.
>
> *Dhammapada 49*

Buddhists recognise that everything changes and that everything depends on the conditions that make its existence possible.

Just as an individual person cannot exist separately from the rest of the world, so the human race cannot assume that the rest of nature and the universe is there for its benefit.

Care for the environment is also a way of following the first two precepts.

▲ Here are some of the jobs that a Buddhist would not want to do

▲ What work would you like to do when you finish your education? What are your ambitions? How do you decide which careers are worthwhile?

Do any of the careers you are thinking of following conflict with the Buddhist precepts?

Buddhism and the Environment

Buddhists try to show kindness towards all creatures. So it is important for them to live in a way that does not damage the Earth. This is how the **sage** (a wise person) should live:

---

1 a) Make a list of occupations that a Buddhist might be happy to follow.

b) Make a list of those that a Buddhist should avoid.

c) As a group, compare your answers. Are there any that you disagree about?

2 Look at the first quotation from the Dhammapada on page 50. What do you think 'he digs up the roots of his life' means?

3 Give examples of actions that a Buddhist would call 'skilful' and others that would be 'unskilful'.

4 Look at the Zen story on page 50. Was Tanzan right to pick up the girl? What do you think he meant by saying that Ekido was 'still carrying her'. What does this story tell you about the Buddhist attitude to rules and regulations?

▲ *These monks in India are studying Sanskrit. This is the traditional religious language of India. Many Buddhist writings are in Sanskrit*

For several hundred years after the death of the Buddha, there were no written scriptures. Stories and teachings were handed down by word of mouth. The earliest Buddhist writings were made on palm leaves, laid on top of one another. They were threaded together with a board placed on top of them to keep them flat.

▲ *A traditional Buddhist book*

Some Buddhists use the same kind of books today. They are often beautifully decorated, and are usually kept wrapped in a cloth to protect them. Of course, there are also copies of the scriptures that are printed and bound like any other modern book.

A monkey king loved his people and wanted to save them. They were being attacked and needed to escape. They tried to cross a ravine, using a creeper as a rope, but the creeper was not long enough.

▲ *A Jataka Tale*

The earliest scriptures were written in Pali, the Buddha's language, and were gathered together in the first century CE. They are called the Tripitaka. This means 'three baskets' and is in three parts:

1 *Vinaya Pitaka* – this contains the rules for organising the life of monks and nuns.
2 *Sutta Pitaka* – this consists of five collections of the teachings of the Buddha.
3 *Abhidhamma Pitaka* – this is the most difficult of the three 'baskets'. It is a collection of Buddhist teachings about the nature of life and is very complex.

Many Buddhists think that the most important of these is the Sutta Pitaka. This includes the Dhammapada, which means 'The Way of the Teaching'. It is one of the most popular Buddhist scriptures, and it is accepted by all Buddhists. Many of the quotations in this book are taken from the Dhammapada.

The Sutta Pitaka also contains a set of stories called the Jataka Tales. Buddhists believe that people have a number of lives before and after this one. Each life produces karma, which affects what happens in the next life. The Jataka Tales claim to

Zen Buddhists do not rely on scriptures, but believe that their traditions have been handed down from teacher to teacher since the time of the Buddha.

Some Japanese Buddhists use koans. These are short phrases or questions which do not seem to make sense. They stop you thinking in the usual way, and force you to use other parts of your mind. You may suddenly 'see' what it is about.

Here is a famous koan:

> What is the sound of one hand clapping?

▲ *One Buddhist teacher was asked if a dog had a soul. He replied 'Mu' – meaning 'No', but he barked it out, like a dog*

The king was tall. He held on to the creeper and made himself into a bridge. The other monkeys ran over him and escaped. His back was broken by the strain. He fell and died.

be about the former lives of the Buddha. They are sometimes about animals rather than people, but they show the sort of life that a person should lead if he or she wishes to become a Buddha one day.

Mahayana Buddhists have other scriptures as well, written in Sanskrit. The most important of these are the Sutras (or teachings). They were written down long after the Pali scriptures. But Mahayana Buddhists believe that they represent genuine teachings of the Buddha.

Like their worship, Mahayana scriptures are colourful and imaginative. In them the historical Buddha is often surrounded by thousands of other Buddhas and Bodhisattvas.

Tibetan Buddhists study the Sutras. Once they have done so, they test themselves by having a **debate**. One person makes a statement. Then his or her partner has to try to find some way to argue against it. This is a good way to make sure that you understand something really thoroughly.

But not all Buddhists read scriptures. A person can learn and put into practice the basic ideas of the Buddhist life without them.

Here is a Buddhist puzzle. You have a goose in a bottle. You cannot get the goose out, without either breaking the bottle or killing the goose. But you do not want to do either. What do you do?

The Buddhist teacher just claps his hands and says 'There! It's out!'

At one level this does not make sense: you can't get it out! But it shows something important. Sometimes life presents you with a problem that you cannot solve by normal means. You worry and worry. Then you suddenly look at life differently, and find that the problem has vanished.

---

1 Look at the Jataka tale at the top of the page. What Buddhist teaching does it illustrate?
2 Take either the one hand clapping, or the dog barking, and explain what you think it means.
3 Working with a partner, choose one idea that you have read in this book. One of you should think of all the arguments in favour of it, the other those against. Then you should try to argue it out between you. This will show you how well you understood the idea.

▲ *Two different images of women in Buddhism: a member of the Western Buddhist Order giving a talk in London and a group of young nuns in Vietnam*

At the time of the Buddha, there were nuns as well as monks among his followers. This was unusual, because in traditional Indian society few women devoted themselves to religion. It was expected that a woman would be a wife and mother.

Buddha taught that women as well as men were capable of enlightenment. But in the scriptures there are some sayings which suggest that men are better able to make progress along the Buddhist path than women.

For many centuries there were no Buddhist nuns, but nowadays there are nuns as well as monks, and they have equal status. A nun may have the title 'Ayya' which means something like 'Sister'.

There are no nuns in some traditionally Buddhist countries today. This is because those societies expect women to live a family life, and not because there is any rule against it in Buddhist teaching.

In Zen Buddhism both women and men can become senior teachers, called Zen masters.

A nun wears robes like a monk, although these are usually a different colour from the men's.

Some British Theravadin nuns wear brown, while the monks have orange. Others have white robes.

Like a monk, a nun has her head shaved as a sign that she has decided to give up family life.

Do nuns do the same work as monks? Do they have the same opportunities to practise their religion? This is what one Theravadin nun said:

> ● The life of the nun is based on the same principles and way of life as that of the monk. In the general running of the monastery, practical tasks are given to whoever can do them, regardless of whether that person is a monk or a nun. For example, both monks and nuns help out with cleaning the monastery and building work.
>
> All those who live in the monastery are given the same opportunities to develop spiritually. The Buddha gave full **ordination** to women and made it clear that enlightenment is available to both sexes.

In the Western Buddhist Order both men and women are ordained. They think that it is less distracting for unmarried members to live in single sex communities and to work in single sex businesses, and enjoy the support that these communities give.

Some Order members have sexual relationships. Some are married with families. However, they claim that it is easier to follow the Buddhist path if a person does not have a family or sex life.

▲ *The Bodhisattva Tara*

Tara is a popular Bodhisattva; she represents the compassion that Buddhists try to develop in their own lives. She is often shown stepping down from her lotus throne. This represents the idea that she is always ready to help those in need.

There is a tradition that Tara went through many different lives. In each of these she chose to be born as a female. This was to help those people who find it easier to respond to a Buddha who is female.

Buddhism often uses the example of a mother caring for her children to illustrate what loving kindness means in practice. One eighth-century teacher argued that if every creature – including ourselves – had been through countless lives before

this one, then every creature must, at some time, have been our mother! It might be difficult to imagine some animal as your mother in a former life. However, the result of trying to imagine this is that you start to have a strong feeling of kindness towards all creatures.

When whales are stranded on a beach, their relatives risk their own lives to join them. It's almost as though they are showing feelings. Buddhists want all creatures to be happy and free from suffering. Remembering the special ties between all mothers and their children helps to promote that.

1 Both Theravadin monks and nuns have robes and shaved heads. Do you think this is a good thing or should women look different? Give reasons for your answer.

2 Make a list of
   a) the qualities that you think of as masculine (e.g. being tough) and
   b) those you think are feminine (e.g. being gentle).
   c) Then, with a partner, compare lists and discuss if each quality is in the right list.
   d) Which of your feminine qualities give you most happiness? (Males should answer this, too.)
   e) Which of your masculine qualities are you most proud of? (Females should answer this, too.)

3 a) Look back at the precepts on pages 48 and 49. List the qualities that you might need in order to keep these.
   b) Do you think it is easier for a man or for a woman to follow the Buddhist path? Explain your answer.

The illustration on page 57 shows the traditional Buddhist Wheel of Life. This is like a map. But instead of showing different countries you can visit, it shows different states of mind in which you can find yourself, and how you can move from one state of mind to another. It also shows things that happen in life and the effects they can have on people.

In the centre of the wheel are three creatures:

- a snake,
- a cockerel
- and a pig.

These represent greed, hatred and ignorance. They are biting each other's tail because they feed on one another.

Around these there is a ring of images, showing six different worlds:

1 The world of the gods, where everyone is happy and life is very refined. Those who enjoy the arts might be quite happy here.
2 The world of aggressive gods, populated by those who are driven to succeed and beat their rivals.
3 Many people inhabit an animal world, and as long as they have enough food, drink, sex and comfort, they ask no more.
4 There are hell realms, both hot and cold, inhabited by those who are depressed or torn apart by hatred.
5 There is the world of 'hungry ghosts', who always want more but are never satisfied. They have knives sticking out of their huge stomachs.
6 Lastly, there is the human realm where people are able to study, think and create.

A person moves from one of these worlds to another. You might know someone who is like a hungry ghost, or someone who is more like an animal than a human being! You might know some people who seem to float around in the world of the gods, for whom nothing ever seems to go wrong. Equally, you might know some aggressive business titans.

On the outer circle are a set of links called the **nidanas**. They are the way the Wheel of Life shows how cause and effect (karma) operates.

First, you are unaware of anything, rather like the blind man at the top right of the circle. Then you start to see things around you. In your ignorance, you want them and grasp at them (much as a monkey might want to grasp and eat fruit as it swings through the trees).

Carried along by your five senses, you may try to grasp at things that you think will bring you happiness. This grasping at the things you see may lead to pain, but perhaps not literally an arrow in your eye!

As you become one with the things you see and want, so you generate karma, which produces yet more life, going on through the cycle of birth and death.

Outside the wheel, there is an image of the god of death, who has his grip on the whole wheel.

But Buddhists see the Dharma as a way to escape from the hatred, greed and ignorance which keep the wheel turning. Therefore, outside the wheel itself is an image of the Buddha, pointing towards an image of a hare in a moon, representing enlightenment.

As you look at the wheel, you might recognise yourself in some of these situations. At different times, you might have been through all of these worlds. They are not just imaginary places in some other universe. They are ways of describing this world, here and now.

1 What might it be like to be someone who is a hungry ghost, never satisfied? Try to describe this situation, with some examples.
2 Buddhists think that it is the human realm that offers the best opportunity to escape out of this wheel and towards a life of happiness.
   a) Why do you think this is so?
   b) Do you think a hungry ghost could escape from the wheel? If not, why not? Why might it be difficult to escape if you are in the realm of the gods?

● Re-becoming

The religion of the Buddha's day, like modern Hinduism, taught that each person had a soul which moved on from one life to another. This is called **reincarnation** or **rebirth**.

The Buddha did not accept the idea of a permanent soul that could move on from one life into another. He thought that we are all made up of various parts, physical and mental, and that these things are constantly changing. He believed that a person's actions (karma) would have an effect on their life in the future.

In other words, things are constantly re-becoming, they are not fixed. But how could what happens in one life influence another life that has not yet started. How could we re-become after death? One way to illustrate this is by thinking of the way in which one candle flame can light another.

Imagine two candles: the flame of one candle causes the wick of the other to catch alight and start burning.

There are now two different flames – one on each candle – but the second is the result of the first.

The Buddha taught that re-becoming worked in the same way: the actions of one life cause things to happen in other lives, and they will go on, even if the first life has ended.

Being born as a human is a rare and precious thing. Imagine a blind turtle, swimming in a vast ocean and surfacing only once every hundred years. A small golden ring floats on the surface. What are the chances that it will put its head up exactly through the middle of that ring? You have the same chance of being reborn as a human. Therefore, wasting a human life is bad because:

- it wastes all the previous births and good karma that led to this rebirth.
- it wastes the chance of getting enlightenment now.
- it wastes the future lives which could build on this one and lead to enlightenment.

Tibetan Buddhists believe that in the case of a few very spiritual teachers (lamas) it is possible to find out who is the new incarnation of that teacher after they have died.

Therefore, when a Dalai Lama dies, there is a hunt for the child that is born as the next Dalai Lama. They put the child to all sorts of tests, seeing if he can pick out the old Dalai Lama's belongings from a pile of similar ones.

Although this may be fascinating, and has sometimes been emphasised in films about Buddhism, it is not the way most Buddhists think about re-becoming.

▲ This is a photograph from a film in which a young boy is thought to be a reincarnate lama. The present Dalai Lama was chosen after a range of tests, although he himself says it was partly by luck!

● Nirvana

The Wheel of Life shows the world of **samsara**, a world in which people are driven on by greed, hatred and ignorance; a world full of changes and suffering.

By contrast, **nirvana** is the name Buddhists give to a situation in which the fires of hatred, greed and ignorance are all put out. Nirvana probably means 'blowing out', because it is the ending of these fires. Instead, a person can live in peace and contentment.

Buddhists believe that they will only achieve nirvana when they finally become enlightened, like the Buddha. Yet, by getting rid of hatred, greed and ignorance here and now, they can experience something of the happiness of nirvana.

> ● Health is the greatest possession.
> Contentment is the greatest treasure. Confidence is the greatest friend. Nirvana is the greatest joy.
> *Dhammapada 204*

Some Mahayana Buddhists suggest that samsara and nirvana are not two different worlds but the same world, looked at in two very different ways. If you are enlightened, you will be in nirvana; if you are hateful, ignorant or greedy, you will still be in samsara.

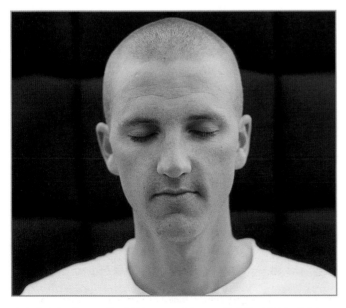

▲ *What is nirvana like? We cannot know. But Buddhists think that by starting to free ourselves of greed, hatred and ignorance, we can experience something of what it is like*

● Don't ask silly questions!

With ideas like 'nirvana' and 're-becoming', you might think that Buddhists spend all their time wondering what will become of them. That's not so. In fact, the Buddha thought that worrying about such things was a waste of time:

> ● This is how he attends unwisely: 'Was I in the past? Was I not in the past? What was I in the past? How was I in the past? Having been what, what did I become in the past: Shall I be in the future? How shall I be in the future? What shall I be in the future? Having been what, what shall I become in the future?' Or else he is inwardly perplexed about the present, thus: 'Am I? Am I not? What am I? How am I? Where has this being come from? Where will it go?'
> *Middle Length Discourses, 2*

In contrast to this, he says that a wise person thinks about the causes of suffering and how to overcome them.

There were many questions put to the Buddha – for example about whether the world is eternal or not, or whether an enlightened person lives on after death – which he refused to answer. He considered that it was simply not helpful for people to worry about such things, the more immediate problem was to overcome suffering and to discover peace and contentment.

1 What three 'fires' are said to be blown out in nirvana?
2 Do you think it is possible to look at the same thing in two completely different ways – perhaps as beautiful but also ugly, or large but also small? Try to think of examples of this. What might a Mahayana Buddhist mean by saying that samsara and nirvana are two different ways of looking at the same world?
3 Explain in your own words why the Buddhist idea of re-becoming is not the same as the Hindu idea of reincarnation, where a soul moves on from one body to the next.
4 Do you think the Buddha was right not to answer some questions? What might have happened if he had given answers to all these things?

● The Bodhisattva Vow

Buddhism helps people to develop compassion towards all creatures. Buddhists do not seek enlightenment just for their own benefit, but for the sake of all beings who have a mind and feelings.

A Bodhisattva is an 'enlightened being'. We have already met Bodhisattvas, since many of the images in Buddhist shrines were called 'bodhisattvas', including, for example, the Bodhisattva Avalokiteshvara (The Bodhisattva of Compassion, see page 36).

By tradition, a Bodhisattva takes a vow to remain in this world in order to help all creatures to achieve enlightenment.

Individual Buddhists can strive to become Bodhisattvas. They can think of themselves as 'apprentice bodhisattvas'. For example, they may want to be like Avalokiteshvara in showing compassion to all.

Can I become like that?

In order to become a Bodhisattva, a person needs to develop six **perfections** which will help him or her in that task. These are seen by many Buddhists as the highest achievement of which a human being is capable. This is how Buddhists present the benefits of developing these perfections:

1 DANA (GIVING)

When you give something, you are sharing part of your life with someone else. You may give someone money or time or energy or friendship. The more you give to people, the more your life is shared with them; you become part of them. In this way people start to live less selfishly, and become aware that their lives depend on many other beings in the world.

▲ *Dana may involve working for others, as well as giving money to charity*

2 SILA (MORALITY)

Following the Buddhist precepts should enable people to get along more easily with others. Being moral and thoughtful in their dealings with others is a good measure of a person's progress!

▲ *The Buddhist view is that **morality** is the result of wisdom. Foolishness shows itself in actions that hurt others*

3 VIRYA (ENERGY)

It's no good just sitting and thinking that it would be good to be enlightened. People need to develop energy to be confident and to do what is right without being afraid.

In the same way, it's not enough for people to think that they should be kind to all creatures;

there are times when you need to show it in practical ways. For Buddhists, action is important as well as meditation.

▲ It is not enough just to sit quietly. Some situations need active help

4 KSHANTI (PATIENCE)

Buddhists feel that it is better to be patient rather than pushing to get one's own way at the expense of others. Rather, people should be kind in all that they do, allowing others their space and responding to them in a positive and helpful way, not in anger.

▲ If your mind rushes off in all directions at once, how can you make progress?

5 SAMADHI (MEDITATION)

Buddhists believe that training and directing your mind is very important.

▲ Being active is one thing, getting frustrated and angry is quite another. You need to assert yourself in a way that helps everybody and that often requires patience

6 PRAJNA (WISDOM)

Buddhists seek to understand the nature of life, the cause of suffering and the way to overcome it. A Buddhist does not think being wise means having a lot of information or reading many books. It is about having a clear mind that can see the truth about life in every situation.

Now I see what it's all about!

▲ Reading; studying; reflecting on your own experiences; being honest about yourself. These are all ways in which Buddhists seek to gain wisdom

---

1 a) Write down each of the six perfections.
b) Give a practical example of each of them. You may either write about it or draw it – but try to give examples other than the ones already shown on this page.

2 Pick any three of the perfections. Explain why you think they are important for Buddhists (think about Buddhist teaching and also the five precepts that Buddhists follow). Then say what value you think these precepts might have for people who do not think of themselves as Buddhist.

Practising Buddhism can be quite a challenge, especially if you live in a society where most people are not Buddhist. The qualities that Buddhists seek to cultivate are not always those of society as a whole, and some people might think them strange for practising meditation or choosing a vegetarian diet.

For those who get ordained as Buddhists, part of that challenge is expressed in terms of a new name. That name is chosen to reflect the person's qualities and is also something to live up to.

We saw Jacques Seneque on page 5. He uses his ordinary name at work, but among fellow Buddhists he is known as 'Satyabandhu'. Here he explains about what his name stands for:

> ● When my teacher gave me my name, he had to explain it to me, because it is in Sanskrit. Satya means 'truthfulness'. Bandhu means 'friend or companion'. So my name means 'companion of truthfulness' or 'true friend'. I think I can be quite a loyal, faithful friend, and I'm interested in the truth. But you've actually got to become your name. It's a reminder of qualities that you need to develop.

▲ *This WBO member wears her scarf only for worship, teaching or meditation. At other times she wears no special clothes*

For further information about Buddhist organisations in Britain, the Buddhist Society, 58 Eccleston Square, London SW1V 1PH publishes the *Buddhist Directory*.

In thinking about what it means for someone to live as a Buddhist, it could be useful to keep in mind the following things, about which Buddhist teachings have something to say:

- War and peace
- Vegetarianism
- Drink and drugs
- Animals
- Craving for things
- Friendship
- Meditation
- Generosity
- Over-indulgence
- Contentment
- The sort of work you do
- Suffering
- The environment

1 a) Write down three things that you think might attract someone in Britain to start practising Buddhism.

b) Write down three things which might make that difficult. (Think about how people live and the ways in which they might need to change if they became Buddhist.)

2 a) Imagine that you have been invited to choose a new name for yourself. What would you like it to be? Remember, like the name given to an ordained Buddhist, it should say something about you, but also something about what you would like to become.

b) Explain how you chose your new name, and how it reflects your view of life.

ascetic – someone who chooses to live by strict disciplines

bhikkhu – Buddhist monks
bhikkhuni – Buddhist nuns
Bodhisattva – 'enlightened being' who seeks to help all others towards enlightenment
Buddha – 'the enlightened one'

compassion – kindness shown to those who suffer
crave – to long for something

debate – argue for or against something
Dharma – the teaching of the Buddha
disciplined – living strictly by rules

elders – senior monks
enlightenment – understanding the truth about life

fast – go without food

Hindu religion – name given to the many ancient religious traditions of India

karma – actions that bring about effects

lay – not **ordained**

mantras – phrases that Buddhists chant
meditation – method of calming and training the mind
metta – 'loving-kindness'; wishing someone well, and expressing it in practical ways
monastic life – the life of monks and nuns
monument – memorial to one who has died
morality – rules or principles to help decide what is right or wrong

nidanas – the links that lead a person from one life to the next
nirvana – a state of perfect peace and happiness in which hatred, greed and ignorance are overcome

ordained – made a member of an 'order', sometimes as a monk or nun or as a member of the Western Buddhist Order. The ceremony for this is called 'ordination'

perfections – qualities to be developed
psychiatry – medical treatment of the mind
puja – Buddhist worship

quest – a task that a person sets out to achieve

Refuges and Precepts – short statement of commitment to the Buddha, the Dharma and the Sangha and to keeping the five guidelines
reincarnation – the belief that a person has other lives before and after this one
relics – the remains of someone who has died
rupas – statues (literally 'bodies')

sage – wise old person
samsara – world of suffering
Sangha – Buddhist community
Sanskrit – ancient religious language of India
scriptures – writings about the Buddhist way of life
spiritual – having to do with personal and religious development
stupas – memorials to the Buddha
symbolic – standing for something else and expressing it

thankas – wall hangings found in Buddhist shrine rooms

viharas – 'resting places'; used of the places where monks and nuns stayed

Wesak – festival that recalls the Buddha's birth, enlightenment and death
wrathful – expressing anger and determination

Index